Breathing Through a Straw

Cody and I

Breathing Through a Straw
Cody and I

Mark William Sheehan

NEW
HOLLAND

Contents

'In the 1950s, children born with cystic fibrosis were not expected to live long enough to attend elementary school.'

Boomer Esiason, former American football player and cystic fibrosis campaigner

Prologue |

As long as I could continue adding pieces to Cody's story as a 'work in progress', I could avoid having to look my life in the eye. Writing this book was, for me, like the tale of the little Dutch boy, who put his finger into a small hole he'd created in the dyke. As long as I kept my finger there, held onto our son's story, I could avoid the emotional floodwaters, and the breaking of the dam.

Like that little Dutch kid, I've clung to the wall, petrified to discover what might happen when I finally do pull my finger out ... looking back, I also may have been, alongside our son, breathing through a straw.

Just keep running, as fast as you can!

As a kid, I won a whopping $10 bet from a neighborhood bully when I flew across the Manhasset Bay 'pluff mud' behind our home. The run could only be attempted during a moon tide. Writing daily about Cody's life was the same for me: as long as I kept flying across the slick, foul-smelling surface, I could avoid sinking into the crap-like gunk.

I made it to shore, covered in repulsive phlegm, and made a 'double-back dare' to the bully who'd baited me: he had to follow my path, or lose face with the other kids along Bay Driveway. When he faltered about 50 feet from shore, he quickly sunk to his knees. The more he wiggled and shook himself about, the deeper and deeper into the pluff mud he went. It was approaching dusk and the tide had turned when we kids on the shoreline realized our local bully was in serious shite. He was 20 yards off and screaming out for help. Joanie Lindner and my kid brother Chris started to cry. We mustered boards and planks and shimmied out to him on our bellies with a rope to tie under his arms. The kid was in shock by this stage, knowing where he was positioned would shortly be under five or six feet of water. With all of us toting, we dragged him to the shore, minus his shoes. The kid was so horrifically ripe, nobody would go near him. The small crater he'd made in the pluff mud was quickly filled with water and vanished.

I feel like that now. If I can just keep running, in my head, I won't sink.

I've always been a sprinter by nature, exploding with bursts of love, and productivity, and gusto, followed by decompressions. I completely collapse on the kerbside, depleted, until I can catch my breath and start sprinting again. My 'old man' used to say I was 'blessed with a short attention span'. When I do get going again, it's often in another totally new direction, along an altogether different path. This personality trait is not conducive to long-term relationships, marriage, or chronicling a tale that runs into decades in the telling. I find it near impossible to revisit or edit anything I've put to paper about my son Cody's journey.

CHAPTER 1 | Thanking You

I sat emotionally devastated, in the office of my publishers, because after more than 20 years of happily calling New Holland Publishers *my* home port, I had all *three* of my proposed book pitches rejected. My pulse went into overdrive, my palms sweated and I dreaded what was coming next.

I knew beforehand that wonderful publishing houses, doing fabulous books worldwide, were closing up shop by the month. Times were viciously tough. But I'd never imagined it would happen to Fiona, New Holland, and *me!* I simply assumed, that Fiona Schultz, powered by her enormous energy and leadership, was going to save us all: our very own Mother Teresa of real, printed books. (She'll scold me for this analogy, but I've bribed my editor in advance to kindly leave it on the page.)

In defending her rejection of my three proposed titles, Fiona said that I'd boldly promised her a bestseller when we first met and my bestselling *America Over Easy!* travel guides 'didn't count'. In her view, I'd yet to deliver the good oil on paper 'as promised'.

Our fabulous Fiona slid a contract face down across her boardroom table, saying, 'This is the book I want this year. It will be the hardest one you have ever done for us. Feel free to take all the time you need … I'll expect it in six months. I want to release it on Father's Day.' The contract was for the story I'd wanted to write for years, and never had the gumption to slip shyly into Fiona's new-books suggestion box. I held back my tears, until I saw hers. Outside her glass office, Lesley, Fiona's good friend and PA for more than 20 years stood crying herself, while offering up a box of tissues.

The 'working title' on the contract read: 'Cody and I: Breathing Through a Straw'.

Dedication works wonders

I truly believe our Cody has come this far, and done this well in large part, because of his spirit and the dedication of his mother. It might be a little bit too far into the telling of this story, but this book is dedicated to Bridget Willis Sheehan, our remarkable son Cody, and to all the other cystic fibrosis kids out there, who continue to press on against some seriously shitty odds.

Today, there are some very smart people within striking distance of a cure for cystic fibrosis. And almost daily now, hope for new treatments and medications is shared worldwide, adding more fuel to the 'find-a-cure' fires. Parents and loved ones, throw emotions and money at lawmakers and health-cover providers by the bucketload to change the lives of CF sufferers. The new treatments and medication band aids are getting better by the week and are available to more kids who need them than ever before. The fighting is far from finished.

CHAPTER 2

Home Is Where the Heart Is!

On the day our Cody was diagnosed, the average life span for a cystic fibrosis kid idled somewhere between 9 and 12 years. Cody is my hero: he's crossed the Rubicon into his thirties, with the help of some remarkably wonderful people. This is Cody's story, and he's given me carte blanche and the blank pages to tell it unencumbered. When I told Cody about 'our book', he said he was 'all-in', but he refused to see the words I'd written until we cut the ribbon at a proper book launch. He hugged me, saying whatever I wrote was going to come from a good place. The kid has a great deal of faith in his father.

In turn, Cody said he'd write 'his bits' and Fiona's team at New Holland Publishers could drop his words into place depending on where they best found a nest alongside mine. Or, better yet, make another book of his view! Our dual apologies in advance for mild redundancies that pop up in our story. Any exaggerations, discrepancies or inaccuracies are all mine.

My son and I made a pact: to not share, or openly discuss this story, until there was no time to turn back. We also agreed that neither his mother, nor his siblings and extended family would have an inkling beforehand.

Cody's story is powerful, and his perch and perspective for telling it is nothing shy of inspirational. Before hitting the print button, Cody asked to have a few of his bits removed for sharing later. When he turns 80! Cody's found his own voice and has many, many more chapters to complete. It's just how the guy rolls. Keep your eyes peeled for his story; he's a wonderful work in progress.

Cody's only caveat

Cody's only proviso to this arrangement was that if our book was to feature photographs, he wanted to have control over any images to be used in the book; he didn't want to discover any full-frontal, butt-naked baby pictures of him in the bathtub with his siblings! He knows me well ... he asked his mom for help when it came to collecting the pictures. Bridget has lovingly documented our entire family journey.

A tear-jerker? Cody won't have a lick of it!

> *'Time spent laughing is time*
> *spent with the gods.'*
> Oriental proverb

Even if I wanted to make Cody's story a tear-jerker, or engage the reader in pulling heart strings, I'm not sufficiently equipped with the writing skills to pull it off. And more to the point, Cody wouldn't have a lick of it.

Cody's story is not like that; from the first contagious belly roll of laughs that popped out of this amazing kid, he set the stage and the tone for everyone who's ever known him, or loved him, or simply enjoyed a brief encounter with this fabulous fella. As a parent, I'm permitted to have a slight bias. Sue me.

Hanging around our son is a bit like taking non-toxic, turbo-charged Red Bull cleverly camouflaged in a quart or two of caffeine: without any of the negative side effects. He's funny, and charming and motivated and, honestly, half the time I don't know where he draws his enormous energy from for pressing ahead with a smile. I light up like a Christmas-tree ornament when I'm around the guy. Cody saved me: most people who know our story mistakenly see things the other way around.

Cystic fibrosis is not contagious – Cody's remarkable lust for living fully *is*!

Childhood – notes in bottles

In 1969 America put a man on the moon, and I drew the not-so-lucky number seven in the US draft lottery for the Vietnam War. My slightly older brother David merrily drew number 330-something the year before. That same year, the planet learned about a magical musical weekend of peace during Woodstock at old man Yasgur's dairy farm. I had a lot to say about it all, but I was unsure of the power of my own, high-pitched and squeaky voice. To let off steam, I began writing haiku-like entries, dating and signing them, and sealing them in bottles. I'd stockpile a dozen or more and then randomly launch them at different shorelines and in surrounding waters to be taken away on the tides. I was writing to an unknown audience of one, whom I'd most likely never meet. It was before 'recycling', and I used bottles that would have layered the Atlantic surface. Most of New York's garbage was being towed and dumped by ocean barges.

I kept a nautical-like logbook in an old ringbinder and recorded the date, the place, tide, and my emotional weather report on the day. I called them my 'float-a-notes', and like snowflakes, no two were ever alike. The places I launched my emotions over the years would make a pincushion of the world map, and those cleansing entries helped me beyond any shrink's sofa, drug, or bottle of grog.

There's a book in those bottles, if I ever get around to writing it. Nowadays, I just write notes to myself on my laptop, and call them by the same name. Some of them have found their way, sprinkled like salt and pepper, into Cody's story. Writing them about our son gave me the chance to put them 'out there' and then move on. Some days it was hard, just getting out of bed. Venting helped.

CHAPTER 3

Getting Started: Charleston, South Carolina

Unknowingly, I started writing *Cody and I* the day I cut the umbilical cord in Charleston, South Carolina, separating Cody from my wife, Bridget. Cody William Sheehan was the most magnificent thing I'd ever seen, created by my beautiful Namibian-born wife Bridget and me. We cried together for this child, counting, through our tears of joy, the fact that he toted the right number of fingers and toes. His limbs were nice and pudgy and Cody's eyes were clear. He inspected his new world and his teary-eyed parents for the first time as though he were sighting a cannon. Cody was taking beautiful, deep breaths, as he practiced using his lungs for the first-ever air outside his mother's womb. We watched him just breathe.

The nurse placed Cody on his mother's chest, while hospital staff morphed the antiseptically spotless delivery room back into a hotel-like suite around us. Oxygen canisters, intravenous drip poles and masks, medical apparatus and other gizmos were all hidden away. You pay extra for this in America.

On the day of our son's birth, my wife and I had unknowingly granted Cody a death sentence. He has the worst genetic combination of cystic fibrosis genes, delivered to him through many previous generations by his genetic family tree. He was created with a many generational Molotov cocktail tossed in that would kill him.

We wouldn't learn this until our son was six months old. Hospitals didn't test for CF at birth in the USA, as they do in many other countries. I'm not sure to this day why. It's a very simple test of salt content – one of the most common elements known to mankind.

Little did I know then that years later I'd become almost immune to the scurry of hospital nurses, interns and intravenous drips, the movement of dinner carts stacked with plastic food and trays, bland blue gowns, and doctors: a seemingly endless ebb and flow of doctors poking our Cody. I've come to detest fluorescent overhead lights.

1989, yep! 'We're pregnant!'

Enlightened with the news that 'we're pregnant', I openly celebrated the fact that I was going to be a father. Inwardly I was scared shitless.

I'm not qualified to speak for other fathers, but I can tell you, when Bridget said that she was pretty sure she had a bun in the oven, I silently went into an emotional tailspin.

While my emotional exterior fuselage appeared to be elated and cruising comfortably at 35,000 feet, the fact was, I needed oxygen. Peter Pan was going to have to grow up, and I was petrified.

I'd never been a father before, but I had a pretty good idea of what the job description was, and the notion of having to care for a child of our own created massive doubts. Could I pull it off, being so accustomed to an emotional 'duck and weave' lifestyle? Confronted with the reality that my life would change forever, I went into tailspins of self-doubt and opened a Pandora's box of petrifying fears. I'd just started a new business, I had no steady prospects or income to speak of, and at the time Bridget was the 'breadwinner' with her job. When Bridget had a baby, all that would have to alter. My headspace got scary, and I started to seriously think about running.

The following morning, I saw Bridget standing in the doorway, modeling her not-yet-showing belly to the mirror, and I knew then it was all going to be fine. Bridget was glowing and happy. I hunkered down to start making a plan. For years afterwards, when things seemed impossible, or impassable obstacles presented themselves, I simply recalled that image of my wife in the doorway of our tiny Charleston cottage, and I could muster the strength to push ahead. Bridget led by unfaltering example, all I needed to do was follow.

Playing with Cody, even before he was born

One of our childhood squat-in-front-of-the-TV programs was *Spanky and Our Gang*. It was always televised in black-and-white, and always anchored in the notion that kids of a feather stick together. We Sheehan kids never had to argue over what channel we wanted when the program aired; it was unanimous among us.

In one of the segments, one of the ragamuffin kids rubbed the belly of his black buddy, 'Buckwheat', suspected of possessing magical powers, while repeatedly making a summer's day wish: 'I wish Cotton was a watermelon!', 'I wish Cotton was a watermelon!' During the segment, the belly-rubber got his wish. (You'd never-ever get away with it nowadays: two black actors, one nicknamed 'Buckwheat' the other 'Cotton'?! In 1960, I recall drinking water in a Greyhound bus terminal in Atlanta, Georgia with a sign over it reading 'Blacks Only'. When I loudly asked our mother what it meant, she quickly shuffled us kids back onto the Florida-bound bus.

When Bridget began to 'show', I'd tenderly rub her watermelon tummy, soothingly saying happy-time things to the baby growing in her belly. I never-once, asked for a 'watermelon'. If Bridget thought this was daft behavior she never said so, and willingly let me have my way with her abdomen. Bridget, in turn, played her favorite music for our belly-bound baby, and for all our future offspring, while she made a nest for each of them inside her.

Bridget flatly refused any alcohol at all during her pregnancies and ate healthful stuff. Not even an aspirin went into her if she could help it. Meanwhile, we occupied a world where you needed to have a drink at hand to be social; Bridget asking for water or juice, in some settings, was considered a slap in the well-heeled ass of our southern hosts. Like a rock, Bridget stood tight and smiled through her champagne flute filled with juice. I tried hard to make up for her antisocial behavior by drinking both our shares of grog! Bridget was a fabulous 'designated driver'. I diligently cut back on nothing, and maintained my weight, and my social drinking, throughout all three of 'our' pregnancies.

Reality hurts!

When I stepped away from the architectural offices of Goff Associates to launch Publicity Plus, I signed Bridget and myself up for a family policy with Blue Cross/Blue Shield. I selected the top coverage for a whopping $300 a month and made certain our coverage included maternity benefits. We were planning ahead.

Bridget's birthing suite was very like a Hilton hotel room: until you noted all the medical gizmos and clinical apparatus hidden behind aesthetically pleasing louvered doors. Tucked in there was all manner of equipment, just waiting for game time. Our coverage paid for two days of this bliss. After that we were on our own for extensions. In the USA, you get tossed out of hospital two days after giving birth, otherwise you pay extra. Lots extra.

A nurse handed me a special set of clipping scissors, and I cut the umbilical cord that connected our son to his mother. I did it though a faceful of tears.

Cody's cat crawls into his cradle

Cody was a smiling, happy baby when we brought him home from the hospital to our cottage in Henrietta Lane, Charleston. Bridget's cat, Gurdy, who'd previously enjoyed full run of the domain, instantly adopted Cody as her own. She would occupy the foot of Cody's crib, which amazed me, as Cody's turds truly ponged, the vapors seemingly able to penetrate leaden walls – an aroma that should have sent up red flags, or rung alarm bells. Poos from un-enzymed CF kids are horrifically ripe. They pong.

We worried Gurdy-cat might accidentally smother Cody, so we made alterations to his crib to safely accommodate her. I was already on the way to becoming a neurotic father, and we planted the crib at our bedside. No need for the high-tech baby monitor. Before Cody was born the cat always took up her place at the foot of our bed on Bridget's side and I would sometimes kick it in my sleep.

Something's just not right

Bridget knew instinctively that something was just not right about our son. She ignored well-intentioned advice about letting Cody cry at night and religiously fed our baby whenever he called out. Bridget extracted breast milk by way of a battery-powered gizmo she attached to her boobs, and when she was too tired to do a 2, 4 and 6 am feeding, I happily fed Cody his bottle from our bed as Gurdy kept vigil, watching me like a schoolmarm, making sure I got the procedure correct.

Our conspiracy to feed Cody was covert, as the experts

kept suggesting that giving in to feeding requests at all hours was setting the stage for a spoiled child. Bridget's instincts have always been good, and I was happy to go along. I have no stomach for the sound of any child crying.

Our baby doctor repeatedly reminded Bridget to just relax; this was, after all, our first child. And 'doctor knows best'.

Bridget insisted that there was something more sinister going on inside of our son, and with dogged determination kept returning to doctors' waiting rooms. When I could, I'd go along to heist a dog-eared copy of the *Reader's Digest*. I've been stealing them from doctors' and dentists' reception rooms since the seventh grade. On the last go-around, the paediatrician said they'd administer a 'salt test' for cystic fibrosis, but she was quite sure this was not what was ailing our son. Looking back, I think she was also already convinced it was a simple case of parental anxiety around a first baby which inspired our many treks to see doctors. The medical community was far too professional and polite to suggest Bridget was being neurotic.

The call that changed it all

I took the call from the doctor's receptionist, asking us to please come to the office after visiting hours, and preferably without Cody. When we arrived after five with our son, the receptionist seemed downright displeased. She'd now have to stay after hours and monitor Cody while we spoke to the duo of doctors in their chambers. I knew something was up. Bridget reluctantly eased over our six-month-old son to the lass at the front desk. The reception area was populated with small, child-sized tables and chairs, and the walls were adorned with smiling turtles and penguins dancing. The floor featured open toy boxes containing hundreds of small, attractively colored plastic pieces that could easily lodge in Cody's throat. I notice things like this. I'm a natural worry wart.

What the doctors confirmed was that, despite their best guesses and earlier notions, our son had tested positive for cystic fibrosis. They tested twice to be certain. The two female practitioners took turns speaking calmly, suggesting that great strides were being made in the treatment of CF. They cautioned us to *not* go looking for answers in the library archives. The information we'd find there was not only out of date, but dreadfully alarming.

Bridget and I, our arms folded in our laps, sat quietly as the doctors spoke. And I could see the teardrops rolling slowly down the cheek of my wonderful wife. I was numb and didn't fully understand what this diagnosis meant down the track. I think Bridget had an unspoken premonition all along. The other thing I recall with great clarity about that day was the weather. It was 98 degrees (37 Centigrade), with almost the same humidity. Our Chevy Nova car had no air conditioning, and I recall being soaked. Looking over at Bridget, I watched a mother hugging her child tightly, all the way home to Henrietta Street.

Cody slept, nested between us that evening instead of in his bedside crib, and we again had Gurdy-cat at our feet, watching over her child. It was the first time in six months we all slept in the same bedding.

I ignored the doctors' suggestion of not doing the homework and, instead of going to the office, I pedaled Bridget's flamingo-pink bike to the Charleston Public Library and peered through the windows, waiting for the doors to open. What I discovered in the literature was devastating ... my beautiful Bridget and I had given our Cody a genetic death sentence; he was not expected to live long enough to attend elementary school. Unknowingly we'd gifted our boy with the dreaded double Delta F508 mutation of cystic fibrosis, the very worst marriage of mutant genes.

Help put us and cystic fibrosis out of business!

On the day that Cody was born, the average lifespan for a CF kid was six to eight years of age, but breakthroughs in the treatment of cystic fibrosis seemed to be cropping up weekly and I was convinced a cure for our Cody was only days away. With the uncovering of the gene that caused CF, came an entire new wave of activities and medications that could improve our Cody's odds.

Bridget and I were keen to do something, so with the help of Bridget's brother Michael in Hong Kong, we imported three, 40-foot containers of furniture and ceramics from the far east, and opened up 7000 feet of retail space along King Street in Charleston, with the sole purpose of raising funds and awareness for CF. We'd never heard of it till Cody was diagnosed with it!

For us, and the baker's dozen college kids who chipped in, we felt every customer held the potential to help find a cure. Some folks spent only a few dollars, while others spent thousands. Even browsers got a flier about CF to take away when they went.

I threw money at a heartfelt TV commercial, solicited the support of the mayor's office, Kiwanis and Rotary clubs, and my buddies at the Hibernian Society passed the bucket around. The newspaper, radio and TV people were all pleasantly in our top pocket.

The night before we opened, we filled galvanized buckets with beer and champagne, and invited the top shelf of South Carolina society to take a sneak peek; black tie, or blue jeans, we took orders on the spot, and promised to deliver the next day. That evening, the till closed at $25,000, with some folks just making a 'small contribution' to the effort, without taking a single thing home but our appreciation. Cody was there, never leaving his perch in Bridget's arms. He was all smiles, and when his Uncle Jim poked his belly, he laughingly poked back.

At eight o'clock on the morning we opened (at 9!), there was a line of 25 people clamoring on the King Street footpath to save 'up to 75 per cent off our products' if they were willing to learn about finding a CF cure. Nobody left our shop without a CF flier.

I've never worked harder, or longer hours on my feet in my entire life. We were open six days a week, from early till late, made free deliveries in exchange for a CF contribution and, in the end, moved over US$250,000 worth of support selling Asian items. Support for CF research and patient services came not only from our customers, but also from wellwishers. We had people ask us repeatedly if we were considering staying in the furniture business full-time and offers to 'sell the franchise' as a money-making proposition. In the end, we kept to our schedule, sold every single bit of inventory we had, and hung a massive THANK YOU! sign in the window when we left.

We had help everywhere we turned. A generous property manager, Colleen, gave us the space for next to nothing, and we in turn said we'd find her a long-term tenant when we left. The Port of Charleston under Bernard Groseclose (our son Dylan Thomas's godfather!) permitted our containers entry without handling fees, the lovable mayor Joe Riley, lieutenant governor, chief of police and other top-shelf locals openly supported our full-frontal campaign for cystic fibrosis, and the Bank of Charleston's Carmel Dodds set up our credit card acceptance and banking 'on the house'. Every member of the Carmody and Griffith family pitched in to help. Both the Rotary and Kiwanis clubs drove clients through our doorway daily and offered to roll up their sleeves as well to help.

Sharing our dream with our community, we discovered we had heaps and heaps of help. I discovered that Bridget and I were not alone in this campaign to see our son, and others with CF, do well. All those generous shoulders to lean into helped me, come out from under the covers.

'Sorry, we're going to have to let you go'

Tonight I pedaled home on Bridget's flamingo-pink beach bike. I'd bought it for her when we lived in Hermosa Beach, mostly because I was attracted to the goofy-fat white-wall tires. I became an 'Injin-giver'* claiming 'back-seize' when I repossessed it to get to work when we moved to historic Charleston. The shocking pink bike was way easy to park, and I rather fancied my image in the handlebar mirror, floating through tourist traffic sporting my Brooks Brothers bow tie and tan poplin suit. At 8 am it was already 75 degrees [24 Celsius] with 85% humidity, and my entire door to door commute took only about eight minutes to accomplish. I couldn't even get the air conditioner in the car to work that fast. Wait up, my car doesn't have air conditioning!

I knew something was up, when I saw Bridget, just in from a full-on day in her office, serving our son his enzyme-spiked applesauce on his gifted sterling baby spoon.

Our loving and larger than life, blacker than coal childminder was wobbling like dark jelly, in tears and shaking like Jell-O at the kitchen sink. Bridget had just fired her. Bridget told me, without breaking stride in her sentences or spooning, that she was quitting her job to stay home. No room for discussion. She would no longer go off to work, while someone else, as loving and kind as they may be, looked after our smiling and CF-laced son.

It was the best news I'd heard in months and I pledged on the spot to do whatever it took to fill the income gaps needed to keep her and our boy out of harm's way. Robbing banks and second-story burglaries could be included in the short list.

*The term was originally granted to the settlers of the US after giving heaps of treaties to the Native Americans, only to ignore them and take lands back later, mostly when they felt like it.

– Journal entry, Charleston, 1989

History and hemorrhoids: foul-smelling turds

In the Middle Ages, kids with 'salty skin' (a telltale sign of cystic fibrosis) died young and were simply considered to be 'bewitched'. Very smelly poos lent support to this notion. In fact, it wasn't until 1936 that a Swiss doctor suggested that what was happening to these kids might just be something more than a bewitching one-off or an isolated occurrence of infant mortality. Nobody even had a clue until 1949 that CF was genetically transmitted by a recessive 'mutant' gene. Or, that it took two to tango; both parents must carry the dormant CF gene to create a child with cystic fibrosis. Neither Bridget nor I had any idea we were toting this genetic baggage around in us until Cody was diagnosed. Neither did any of our ancestors, apparently. Looking back over family archives, child deaths were usually attributed to pneumonia or cot death, or …

Thank God for applesauce

Long before anyone knew about cystic fibrosis, another life-enhancing discovery for our son Cody was made. In medieval times somebody pummeled the hell out of ripening apples, added a bit of sugar or cinnamon, and converted them by the bucketload into a paste. In the early 1700s, the recipe was enhanced and the lass who penned *The Compleat Housewife* highlighted the details of how it was done. Being a Pilgrim, she simply called it 'apples in a sauce'. It was the first cookery book to be published in the original thirteen colonies of America and, oddly enough, also contained the first published recipe for 'katchup'. The author suggested using the mush of beyond-ripened tomatoes alongside pork roasts. A condiment trend that endures to this day. One hundred years later, the Gerber family baby foods company discovered they could successfully sell mushy apples in tiny jars, small enough to fly a teaspoon into. Modern mothers took the bait, hook line and spoonful, and landed millions of spoonfuls into the mouths of their babies.

Bridget relished the variety of choices in those little jars when she discovered Cody loved the apple sauce. By hiding Cody's much needed pancreatic enzymes in smooth apple sauces, he could more pleasantly absorb nutrients, and digest meals and calorie-packed milkshakes better. And the tiny little jars and caps made great recycled depositories for my notes in bottles.

Bridget's discovery also meant that Cody's turd deposits were far more evolved, and not as ripe as when we had to change loaded, and nearly undigested, diapers. Thankfully, Cody took to devouring his enzyme-laced apple sauce and baby food with a smile. Because cystic fibrosis kids don't digest food fully, they become malnourished. Taking enzymes is a bit like feeding hundreds of tiny depth charges to a CF child, which explode in the digestive tract and help convert foods to nutrients. Because Cody was too tiny to swallow the capsules whole, Bridget would open each one, sprinkle and mix them like salt into the applesauce, and spoon feed him. This often took hours, and Bridget always made certain Cody didn't see mealtimes as a chore. If you tallied it up, mother and son would have spent years together, playing at the dinner table. If Cody had refused to eat, we'd have been forced to have him take his meals via a belly pump and to that point we'd not had to poke any permanent holes in our son that weren't already there.

(Cody's only known rebellion to taking enzymes occurred when he was starting pre-kindergarten at the Farmhouse Montessori School in Sydney. I only learned this years after the event from his best-ever school-buddy, Jasper. I was in London at the time, or Boston, or maybe New York … Apparently, Cody crossed his arms, on day one in front of the entire class, stubbornly refusing to swallow a single tablet, until his new pal Jasper stepped in and popped one into his own mouth leading by example. Wilma the teacher stood in shock as other kids in Cody's class lined up, volunteering to try one too. Cody never resisted taking enzymes after that episode. He's become so good at covertly taking four, six, and sometimes eight at a meal that I can no longer observe the process. Bridget and Jasper's mom, Lilly, each got a call at home from Wilma to discuss the potential toilet-bowl ramifications of the event. Our families have become wonderfully melded ever since. We adore them all.

Other CF kids, not as keen to get stuck into their mushy meals as Cody, were being kept going, treading the edges of nutrition via tube feeding. Some simply couldn't keep food down, and the notion that every mealtime meant a serious puking, was not an attractive option around any CF family dinner table.

Many years later one of Cody's good pals (they met on the children's hospital ward at Randwick in Sydney) had to actually be taught how to chew and swallow real food after his successful transplant. He'd been fed via a tube his entire life. He was 12 when he had his first backyard hamburger. I learned recently from his mother that he was playing soccer on the weekends and had himself a real girlfriend too.

Hurricane Hugo

Twelve hours before Hurricane Hugo made landfall and devastated the city of Charleston, a military half-track loaded with fully armed National Guardsmen and local police toting bullhorns rolled through Henrietta Street, demanding we evacuate. It was not a request. The highest point in town was a mere 13 feet above sea level, and the possible storm surge could easily double that depth. Bridget and I threw Cody's nebulizer machine, the big cooler bag to store his refrigerator necessities, family photo albums, Gurdy-cat and other irreplaceable items into our station wagon and moved other things we couldn't tote up to the second floor. Bridget filled the three claw-footed bathtubs to the brim with water, an act I thought odd at the time. We left Bridge's Chevy Nova parked in our driveway – the car was later lifted up and re-parked by the tidal surge, lodged sideways. About 40 feet away from it was a 28-foot sport fishing boat, both its massive outboard motors dangling from the hull like mobiles. Every lane of the interstate was pointed inland; if you wanted to go into town, you'd have to be driving in the median strip. Militia lined the roadway every mile or so.

We took the back roads out of the city, going inland to our weekend fixer-upper on Christmas Place in Camden, South Carolina. Camden, a historic town and home to the Carolina Cup horse races, is 127 miles (204 kilometres) inland from Charleston and we wanted to be safe. As quietly as I could, I dragged the spare mattresses off the guest beds, lined the walls of our walk-in closet, and drew a tarp over the clothing rails to create a makeshift roof for my family. We were over two hours from the coast and, even here, I was certain the hurricane would find us and tear the roof away. Trees were being bullied around by the wind, and 100-year-old magnolias were sheering like toothpicks around us. The pine trees had already snapped hours earlier. The white picket fence at the front was blown miles away. Armour-piercing rain flew sideways, seeming to never touch the ground.

Cody was at Bridget's side for the entire time, both sleeping soundly while I shunted furniture in the dark; powerlines had gone down two hours earlier. And I counted my steps, practicing the distance between the bed and the cavern I'd created in our closet. Remarkably, Bridget was sleeping soundly through the hurricane while trees were snapping, roofs rattling free from their joists and rain making the thunder of a dozen freight trains, Bridget slept soundly … *until* … the very first whimper from Cody and his need for a night-time feeding. My wife's hearing had pin-drop clarity when it came to her son. I think it's true: if you live near railway tracks for long enough, you never again hear the train.

It was a full three days after the hurricane before residents of peninsula Charleston were permitted to return to the city. National Guard roadblocks confirmed our address, allowing us to pass. Only vital services being the exception. Looters traveled via backyards and on foot to get to the storefronts on King Street …

The kindness of strangers

I walked into the Federal Building on Meeting Street, normally an easy stroll along a tree-lined laneway. Now splintered and ruined trees were splayed along the path, massive tree trunks and limbs akimbo like giraffes spread-eagled at a watering hole. I had been given good hiking boots by Bridget for Christmas and appreciated them with every step of the 100-yard trek.

The Federal Building was lit like a Rockefeller Center Christmas tree, while the rest of the city was in total darkness, and I needed power desperately to keep Cody's 'liquid gold' medications cold, and to operate the masked nebulizer that he required three times every day to just break even on the suffocating mucus flooding his lungs.

I was whipping myself internally, as I'd made the poor choice to leave our powerless bivouac in Camden, in the hope of having power and water in Charleston. I was dreadfully worse off for the decision. Bridget and Cody were fully spent, the trip had been horrific, and we arrived to a darkened historic city, corners monitored by fully armed and flak-jacketed National Guard soldiers to prevent looting. The first shots of the Civil War were fired from Charleston's ramparts, and the damage might have been similar.

We'd been living in our Ford ('Fix Or Repair Daily') LTD station wagon, running the engine and using the cigarette lighter adapter for Cody's air pump, and when I explained this to the three fellas behind the counter in the FBI office, I was crying openly. I was furious with my bad call, fully frustrated, and I simply abandoned any pretense of keeping myself together. I pleaded with them to kindly keep Cody's medicines I had tucked under my arms in their refrigerator. I started shaking uncontrollably, trying to ask if I could bring my son up the path for his nebulizer needs. I later learned, every one of those FBI agents who witnessed my breakdown were fathers.

I'd finally come apart, sobbing into my palms, and collapsing into a plastic Kmart chair previously occupied by the security guard. Minutes later, I was force-fed a cup of strong coffee, while it appeared an entire army of agents and administrators began to string a mile-long orange power line the length of a football field directly in through our living room window. We had the fridge running, a heater on full tilt as Bridget's feet, and Cody's facemask at premium performance. I was still crying, only now, my tears were dropping for kinder reasons as I hugged everyone in arm's reach. I loved those guys between Kleenexes. The FBI crew also chipped in to help a FEMA (Federal Emergency Management Agency) team to rig up a switching station at the foot of our driveway – a temporary power pole, so the five other homes on Henrietta Street also had power. John, the chain-smoking lead agent had three young kids of his own at home 'up north', and showed me pictures from his wallet while emergency services buzzed around us. He hadn't seen them in days, unsure of when he'd be able to return home.

Cody laughed, and smiled, and beamed at all the commotion, thinking perhaps that this was simply another marvelous game staged for his enjoyment. Years later I asked, and he recalled nothing of the event, but then again, he was just nine months old, still in very smelly nappies: like most other CF kids who made it that far.

Surrounded by lovely historic homes and antebellum architecture, I used to curse the concrete, ugly-looking and antiseptic Federal Building's facade. After Hurricane Hugo, when I passed by, I would think that it was the home office to some of the most unexpected and compassionate people that have ever populated the planet. My faith in the goodness of others was given a wonderful emotional booster shot.

Once every month or so for years afterwards, I'd happily hand deliver a basket of fresh fruit or chocolates to that office – even though most of the FBI agents and people who helped the Sheehans survive Hurricane Hugo were long returned to their families. With every delivery, I shared a story of kindness, passed along with our son Cody's best wishes. What goes around, comes around.

The 100-year snow and not a single day off

I stood at our bedroom window with tiny Cody in my arms, watching Bridget make a snowball in our garden. Snow in Charleston was a fluke of nature, and Bridget, wrapped in my goose-down jacket, was making the most of it. She lay on her back, beaming up at Cody and me, making angels in the snow, and tossing quickly constructed snowballs at the window. Cody laughed from his very core with each toss. Even with the window closed, I could hear the sounds of cars colliding on Calhoun Street; southerners simply don't know how to drive in the snow!

It was the first time I took notice of the fact that Bridget had been with Cody almost constantly, for months on end. Her brief snow-time playing about reminded me of a clip I saw that went viral on YouTube. It was a video capturing the antics of milking cows that had been pent up for an entire lifetime in the barn. When the heifers were let loose into a green, sun-filled pasture they actually leapt, danced, pranced, preened each other and strutted around, wrapped in their new freedom. If cows could smile, they did.

Bridget came indoors, soaked to the bones and beaming. With a small CF child under our roof, freedom came to Bridget in very small doses, and I made a note to myself to give her and Cody some time to play. Apart.

There are thousands of CF parents and loved ones out there, marking time for a cure or better treatments to be discovered, and I compliment them all. Unless you've ever lost a limb or had a loved one with cystic fibrosis or another chronic childhood illness, I'm guessing it's hard to get any traction for how it feels every day when you try to put a positive foot on the floorboards. In that first year, I think I could count on two fingers the belly laughs I heard from Bridget when she was more than 20 feet from our son. The day of the 100-year snow was one of them.

Can we do this? Can we even AFFORD this?

With her daily digging into new developments in the treatment of cystic fibrosis, Bridget would deliver facts and encouraging news over our wobbly dinner table. Cody smiled happily, nestled between us in a well-lined wicker picnic basket. Cody, in the basket, sat atop my homemade dining table, while Gurdy-cat sprawled out there as well. I'd built, sanded, and then varnished the table out of necessity. I scrounged up timber off-cuts and married them to each other with commercial-grade flooring glue. There's a good reason they call the stuff 'dope'. The entire table was held together with a dozen discarded galvanized nails: instead of proper fastenings and screws, I'd used whatever I could find at arm's length.

Oddly enough, our newly found Charleston friends boasted big lawns, four bathrooms, and handed-down antiques. These young couples owned crystal glassware and sterling silver cutlery. Our bookshelves were still upturned wooden milk crates. Both Bridget and I were late bloomers, and we must have appeared to be quite bohemian

When I began looking into the numerical facts about our Cody's cystic fibrosis, some alarming numbers slapped me in the face. In addition to the shockingly sad life expectancy of a CF child, the fact was that the cost of simply keeping a CF patient treading sputum was a whopping $US80,000 plus a year. I was both shocked, and inwardly relieved. I'd already signed up for family cover of the best reputation. I'd set up top-shelf Blue Cross Blue Shield family coverage even before Cody was born, when I launched my new PR business, Publicity Plus. I figured, even if I had to belly-up to the bank window for the first $5000 deductible required each year, we'd be home free after that with Blue Cross having my back.

My Rolls Royce choice of health cover was going to look after our family's medical mountains, and I emotionally patted my posterior for spending a bit more on the monthly premiums. I began to sleep a wee bit better knowing that Blue Cross Blue Shield would be there supporting us for the *big* outstanding balances, covering the remaining dollars needed for Cody. As long as we paid our premiums on time each month, and didn't miss an invoice beat, we would be comfortably covered.

Bridget, who looked after all our banking and bills from the start of our new public relations business, had a crystal-clear mandate from me: There were *two* bills that must always be paid on time. We could *never*, as in *ever*, let either my life insurance policy or, our Blue Cross bills lapse. I think it's my own phobia, even if there's not a Latin name for it. I painfully recalled my own mother's financial agonies when our father died suddenly, leaving behind six kids, a home on Manhasset Bay with a clay tennis court, a two-masted schooner, and no life insurance to pay for playing with any of it. It was not going to happen on my watch.

I'd taken my term life policy out when I was only 14,

listing my mother as sole beneficiary, and the skinny-ass premiums were marginal for a whopping-big payload. When my mother died, and I later married Bridget, I simply swapped the beneficiary's name, and paid the same low premiums. Years later, when it did lapse, the cost of getting the same value at my age was exorbitant and fully out of my financial reach.

I reminded Bridget repeatedly that our medical plan coverage at Blue Shield, like my term life policy, was the new cream; even if it meant being late for mortgage payments, credit cards, electricity, or the whopping-big phone bills. Everyone, even our corner grocer, would have to wait behind my term life and the boys at Blue Cross cover.

Life on hold – a new plan

Bridget gave up her aspirations to act, a creative passion for pottery and sculpting, and a vibrant travel career. And her income: she pledged herself to stay fully focused on giving our son every chance possible in life. A massive commitment on her part, with no escape clauses to looking after the home-front hive. All that I had to look after was bringing home the honey.

Blue DOUBLE-Cross and Blue NO-Shield insurance?

All was swell, until the health insurance company began to reject co-payments. After Cody was diagnosed, my relationships with our insurance providers changed dramatically. Instead sending me checks for their portion of medical bills, I began getting notices headed 'refusal to pay' and declining and denying all future claims. I began getting mass-produced letters informing us that Cody had a 'pre-existing condition' and it appeared they were saying, all bets were off.

After my 'top shelf' insurance provider notified me by form letter that Cody was not covered I went into an emotional nosedive. I had painstakingly filled out dozens of forms and made claims, which in return became rejection slips dropped through our letterbox. They were all the same, only the specific reference numbers were changed. My insurance 'providers' lied. No-one signed the letters; they were, all of them, generically ended. Cowards. Time and again they would deny and decline and rubber stamp without a shred of emotion or compassion. Just rubber-stamped rejections.

I kept this bankrupting bad news from Bridget, who was sleeping snugly with Cody tucked alongside her at night or sleeping with the crib by her side of the bed for nocturnal feedings on demand. Gurdy slept as a sentry at the foot of the cot. I was again doing agonizingly sleepless nights, and if the truth be known, delivering a less than stellar performance for my new public relations clients.

I was quietly drinking during the day to take the edge off; not enough to hamper my ability to drive at the drop of a sombrero, but it was an activity I'd never undertaken before. My drinking had evolved from only on weekends to only tampering with the toxins after work, but now I was joining some of my low-country peers in the pub at noontime. I was quietly slinking off around the corner to Agostino's and playing Pac-Man for hours on end. Nothing escapes Bridget, who had childhood experience in spotting the signs, and she let me know that I was not really flying well under anyone's radar.

When I got the thirteenth or maybe fourteenth form letter, claiming that Cody's condition was 'pre-existing' I wept openly. I had been lied to and betrayed by faceless employees in far-off corporate offices and I wanted revenge. For the very first time, I had a sense of why a veteran postal employee in Florida, after years of on-the-job abuse, marched into his former employer's office with a pistol and began firing. When he was finished, and had exhausted his rage, he put the gun to his head. I hosted a true hatred for people I'd never even met, and I could taste the vengeance that bullied postal employee must have felt in those last moments.

A month earlier, on the heels of Hurricane Hugo, our home was robbed. Along with other items, both my double-barreled shotgun and Smith & Wesson target pistol were stolen from the back of my closet. Instead of replacing them with the insurance money, Bridget and I bought a new side-by-side refrigerator. (Nine weeks later, I learned my guns had been used in a robbery attempt at a 7-Eleven store in Sumter, South Carolina. They were going to be 'held as evidence' for the trial. A form accompanied the letter, asking me if I'd like to recover the weapons, and I ticked the box to have them melted.)

Thankfully, my rage was confined to indoors, where I created a sizable hole in my new sheet-rocked wall, while vowing to go down fighting, with venom in my fangs. Bridget, seeing the hole in the wall, simply leaned into me with a hug, Cody nestled in her arms between us. She was my rock, reminding me I'd find my way through it.

Deny, deny, and then, when all else fails ... deny!

To launch a counterattack, I recruited a fella who was well equipped to help me inject my venom. I reached out for the street-smart skills of my friend and lawyer, 'Rusty' Bennett. Rusty's firm was my client at Publicity Plus, and his firm thrived on gutting insurance companies. Sort of a male version of Erin Brockovich, Rusty went into the batter's box for us like the legendary 1950s New York Yankee's slugger Yogi Berra, with an eye on the World Series. Our panzer attack was created with the intention to either force a reinstating of medical coverage for Cody or turn my crusade into a national incident with a whopping big payout. Rusty's creative correspondence was remarkable, and a paper trail of 'certified letters', 'return receipt required' and other clever tools of the legal negotiating trade set the stage for a 60 Minutes TV special on the subject. Through 'discovery' Rusty was able to identify and reveal the names of the real people on the other end of the faceless rejections. Board members and investment funds who held stock in this outfit were copied in on the correspondence. Some of these went to board members' front doorstep at dinner time.

In the end, the insurance underwriters offered me a 'significant settlement' to relieve them of any obligation, by way of a 'generous offer of $150,000'. I asked Bridget what she thought about caving in for the cash: I was so exhausted with the constant emotional hemorrhage that I was truly tempted to toss in the towel and take the money. But CF isn't a cheap date, and Bridget reminded me of the math, and our promise to get Cody well into his old age. She calculated that the money would give Cody a little over two years of care.

Bridget's reply was like a dagger's blade rammed into my middle. 'Mark! Are you willing to agree with the bastard insurance company that Cody is only going to live two to three years?! Because that's what they are offering us to slink away, and it cleverly has a hidden gag order attached to it?'

After a short pause, and regaining her composure, Bridget continued, 'Mark, how many other families are they doing this to? When you look at what the cost is to get our boy to the age of 21 … we are not in this alone.'

Her words cut into me because she was simply prodding me with a pitchfork, dipped in the truth.

We rejected the offer, and although we had to drop all the other family coverage in the years following, we were at least able to hold their feet to the fire financially for a big chunk of the funds we would need. The future prospect of Cody's medications costing over $100,000 each year left us no choice.

Fighting back – I have no stomach for confrontation

The fight path we took was emotionally crippling for me: a saga I'd not care to share, other than to say it was heart-wrenching. I'd have preferred to give up, but at each turn of the screws, when the latest setback suggested I should just cave in, the sight of Cody in the rocking chair with his mother empowered me. Each week bought to our front door another seemingly impossible hurdle or barrier to climb. When it was all over, Rusty refused to take a penny: instead, he demanded a hug and a cold beer from our new fridge, which I delivered in tears. The guy is a candidate for cloning.

Death by 1000 stab wounds

In the end, while we were 'allowed' to continue Cody's coverage, what Blue Cross Blue Shield did afterwards, although deplorable, was in keeping within the 'letter of the law': they increased my premiums at every lawful opportunity, making us pay the ever increasing premiums annually. I understand they use this wedge frequently, the bastards. We were locked into ever-increasing premiums and US$10,000 to $20,000 annual deductibles. Like the guy who had been robbing 7-Elevens across the state with my stolen shotgun, I considered the possibility of robbing a bank.

When we later discovered, or supplemented Cody's treatments and meds with promising items that were not yet approved by the Food and Drug Administration, these cutting-edge meds we paid for fully at our own expense. Bridget would say with a smile that we'd be eating lots of spaghetti bolognaise and hot dogs for a while.

The reality that I was unable to afford our full family coverage sent me into tailspins. I was confronted with the harsh reality of the dollars and we dropped both Bridget and me from the insurance policy, clinging desperately to Cody's cover. Even when it meant missing mortgage payments.

We scrambled madly for other dollars to access medications and seek the best care for Cody-son. The monthly cost climbed into the thousands and the invoice for the emotional damage under our roofline was beyond measuring. In my head, I was the breadwinner who could not provide the bread.

Around this same time, I quietly upgraded the payouts for my term life insurance, with an eye towards safeguarding our son's future if I kicked the bucket.

Short of cash? Maybe you should rob a bank!

I started looking around for a way to supplement our cashflow. An old rule of thumb amongst bank robbers was that they could get away with about three robberies before they were caught; similarly, 20 burglaries before apprehension.

For a time, I'd considered if I might alter my professional career path to advantage, when reality slapped me across the tallywhacker. It was clear I'd need to unearth at least $80,000 a year to toss at health care, and with Bridget's wonderful promise to pull the plug on her aspirations until we got Cody on the right path, we'd not be able to count on a dual income for a time.

I took the logical of step of learning a new trade: how to rob banks without being caught. My wake-up call came when one of our drinking pals at the Hibernian Society (the oldest in America) back bar, from the sunshine state of Florida, was arrested for robbing 11 banks in the last 8 years. He'd picked his targets carefully, determining first which locations had the least amount of coverage for the FBI, and the farthest travel times between federal offices. If agents doing investigations had to be away from home for long bouts, his odds of staying under the radar increased significantly. His comment from lock-up was that he always knew he'd eventually get caught, it was just matter of living well, spending up, and putting some in a safe place for when he'd done his time. Good bank robbers take months, planning a heist to advantage, and we had often wondered around a pint of beer, why his business interests would keep him out of Charleston for such long bouts. His arrest was a wake-up call.

Our mother's words came back to me from my childhood: 'What on earth, were you thinking?!' She made the inquiry after my brother and I hot-wired a bulldozer on a dare, taking out a dozen trees before we figured out how to stop the thing in its tracks. We'd just moved into the neighborhood, keen to make friends with the other kids.

Boomer's boy Gunner and Ronald McDonald House

It was to be the first of many treks for us to clinics around the world. Things were, happily, changing rapidly for CF sufferers, and we visited clinics that melded into family holidays or my work agenda. Over the years, we have strung CF clinics together like a pearl necklace in more than 24 cities.

Charleston, South Carolina has been on the *Condé Nast Traveler* top-10 list for years as a spectacular city to visit, but it was not the best nest for a family coping with a genetic illness like cystic fibrosis. Bridget quickly assessed the well-intentioned but unenlightened local pool of medical practitioners and aggressively began making plans to seek help elsewhere outside the city limits.

Bridget discovered that the best clinic for CF kids within a day's drive from Charleston was in Winston-Salem, North Carolina, and we made a number of road trips there to get Cody properly evaluated. We also discovered other CF families to share our unspoken thoughts and fears with, nesting nightly in Ronald McDonald House, where we enjoyed endless access to the refrigerator, home delivery of burgers and fries (even the costume-clad Hamburgler made home deliveries here!), and fabulous local goodwill from volunteers with sympathetic ears.

Cody played alongside smiling cancer kids, chased balloons around an ample playroom, watched *Thomas the Tank Engine* on TV, and had no idea that according to the numbers, statistically, he'd be the first fatality among the kids in the room. We read Cody books at bedtime, all of them with happy endings. None featured kids on chemo, extended families crying openly in foyers for the loss of a four-year-old, or doctors toting clipboards in blue open-backed scrubs delivering postmortems to sobbing mothers.

Cody, in the company of body casts and chemo kids played happily on the indoor monkey bars and swings. These sick kids shared spit and smiled and inhaled every good thing about being sick. Caring parents helped, or hovered nearby like school-dance wallflowers. The power of a child smiling is motivating, particularly when some children appear to have absolutely everything to cry about. The smile from a small child should be enough to move an entire mountain range. Chronically sick children moved my world to a much better place than I'd ever experienced before. I started hugging other parents without even knowing their names. They seemed to 'get me'.

'Boomer' Esiason, a famous American football quarterback, and his CF son Gunnar, were among them. Boomer Esiason is a former American football (gridiron) quarterback and sports analyst with CBS Sports Network who played in the National Football League for 14 seasons. He is a well-known Superbowl combatant. When our kids first met, I was unaware that Boomer lives in Manhasset, Long Island, my childhood stomping ground.

CF kids seem to have been given, genetically, more smiles than the rest of us! A mixed blessing: lungs are usually the first organs to go off, followed closely by a kid's liver, kidneys and a massively swollen and painfully puffed-up spleen. Cystic fibrosis children may look like poster kids on the outside, while their innards progressively rot away.

Sometimes the diabetes they most likely develop if they live long enough to become teens kills them.

One of the most intriguing things about Cody's contagious good vibe is that he's not really that unique among his sphere of CF friends. Cody's other 'cystas' and 'fibros' I've come to love seem also to possess an extra magical 'mutation' – without exception, these CFers are built to be stronger than the rest of us.

Dedication works wonders

Every day. Having a child with the Delta F508 CF gene meant there was never really a day off for Bridget. The dedication it takes to spoonfeed up to 40 pancreatic enzymes to an infant through applesauce or thump a child's small frame to break up the goo which constantly coats the lungs, absorbs up to four hours of daylight. At least four hours. We were lucky enough with Cody's treatment to be able to put some remarkable meds into his nebulizer, which added, easily, another two hours of attention to this smiling kid every, single day. I'd help with this when I was home, but I was often away for weeks on end.

Who's counting?!

On 3 February, Cody's birth date, the colony of Massachusetts issued the first paper money in America. The year was 1690, and the event changed lives forever. Cody's birthday in 1989 changed mine.

Bridget was relentless in chasing the latest information and breaking news on medical advancements in cystic fibrosis research and chewed up the information like a blender. It seemed almost weekly there was a crack in the shell, offering up new hope. The bottom line was, there was hope, and we were not alone in our dream for better treatments and, one day, a cure. New, experimental, and early-stage treatments were available for our Cody; all we needed to do was rob a few banks to get at them.

Bridget created our very own underground railroad, and we imported medications that had not yet been Food and Drug Administration 'approved' or were not reimbursable by any medical plan. All we needed to do was ensure they were refrigerated from dispensary to doorstep. And belly-up with the bucks to pay for them in advance.

There's an entire underground army of them

Cody and his other CF 'cystas' and 'fibros' continue to inspire, enlighten and motivate me on a daily basis. The planet is blessed for having them on it. Our challenge is to keep them with us for as long as possible. And find a cure. CF sufferers often seem to be gifted with special powers – Cody happily calls himself a mutant 'CF Avenger'. And when I think about it, he's right on the money. The Marvel Comics superheroes are all mutants, genetically altered characters. I shed tears when I see the support they lend to each other. It's mostly non-physical nowadays because of the need to keep their distance and avoid cross-infections. The rule of interaction is at least five-feet apart at all times.

There is still no cure for CF, or our handsome son. Yet we've uncovered an entire army of wonderful people, each one willing to do whatever it takes to make sure Cody and other CFers like him, breathe to the best of their ability. We're never really alone now. The power of a small child's laughter, our child's small belly-roll of giggles, got me laughing and living again. Cody continues to be my hero. I'm hoping that in some small way, this book will reach out and touch others, the way the laugher of a small child, my Cody, reached out and saved me. I am blessed beyond any tool ever invented for measuring.

That was over 25 years ago now. In part, it was the power of our son and the smiles he held on his face that pushed me from under the covers and made me clear the bedroom threshold. My wife helped me up, and together we were determined to defy all the odds that seemed to be stacked against our boy.

CHAPTER 4

Before Bridget |

For years before I met Bridget, I was dedicated to the notion of remaining single. With my five fantastic siblings all, fully loaded with walking, crawling proof of their ability to carry on the Sheehan family gene pool, I was committed to avoiding the marriage wading pool entirely. I was gladly going to remain in the marital shallows, wading only up to my ankles and, if necessary, taking dips into transient partners for as long as I was able to breathe freely.

I was going to be the 'incredible Uncle Mark'! The Uncle Mark who spoiled his nice nieces and numerous nephews to bits. As an adventure-seeking nomad, I'd plan to pop into my siblings' guest quarters, rejuvenate my batteries at their wonderfully loving and gracious hearths, enjoy savory home cooking and loving camaraderie, get my laundry and banking done, read my mail … and then, vanish. I could abuse the dishwasher cycle and overflow the clothes washer (to my credit, I only flooded the entire basement of David and

Ellen's home once!) and then I'd simply light out to the next adventure. I was very good about writing clever, educational postcards to the kids from the Grand Canyon, or Kenya, or beyond.

I'd buy and build right from the box, a baker's dozen first bicycles ('some assembly required' are words that should be stricken from the language!), which the recipient kids invariably broke limbs attempting to tackle.

I was the uncle who bought and then constructed (over a six-pack of beers before breakfast) a significant backyard swing set: my nephew fell off the slide on the very first day of its ribbon cutting and broke his leg; and the 'Uncle Mark!' who bought a shiny pink bike, which required an engineering degree to assemble, only to have my very nice niece break an arm on her maiden voyage.

My bad. Okay, so I was meant to be holding Meghan (aka 'Meggler-Peggler'!) upright in the new bike's saddle, when childhood flashbacks of pushing my kid sister Cathy into poison ivy paused me dead in my flip-flops. Meghan got more than halfway down the block, gaining speed, before she fell. I'd earlier carefully discarded the dozen 'extra' washers and nuts leftover from my assembly effort … which I learned later were needed for the brakes. I'm not very good on following directions. Printed or verbal. I've also got a problem with authority.

I raised some serious eyebrows among my siblings, who cheerfully repeated the mantra, 'Come often, stay as long as you please and bring only board games into the house from now on.'

I could pamper my multiple nice nieces and nephews, apologize to their parents for the occasional cast or cosmetic stitches on one of the kids and leave a gift certificate for Lobster Hut under the recliner chair in the TV room for the family to enjoy in my absence. It's important to say 'thank you'.

The lure of the open road spoke to me: I was for all intents and purposes a modern-day Peter Pan, happily roaming without the participation of a full-time Wendy on board. Leading treks for six months, married to seasonal overseas sales and marketing assignments, meant that I was able to remain a pleasant, and ever-moving emotional target. With three months off a year to spend in Spain, or Mexico, or Africa or …

My brilliant brother David and his wonderful wife Ellen took the brunt of my nomadic invasions and added advice alongside Ellen's great spaghetti and homemade meatballs. To this day, David is still collecting and advising on my mail, forwarding the important stuff, dumping the junk, and continuing to keep me out of harm's way. David is a brilliant Tinker Bell to my Peter Pan behavior. He still looks after me and he's always had my back.

Being the good brother, and an even more generous uncle, I'd occasionally 'step up' and take out the garbage or change seriously smelly nappies. I like to think I was a pretty good babysitter. My family was unconvinced I'd ever snap out of it, and openly prayed I'd settle down one day. Relatives dropped hints like breadcrumbs for me to follow; I just was not in a place where I wanted to be looking down.

Playing at marriage

When I met Bridget in Cape Town, I was told straight up by the fella who introduced us, Silvio Barretta, to steer well clear. Bridget was totally and fully off limits. She was way too wonderful for me to be playing a trek leader's 'plow and go' routine on. As a diversionary tactic, Silvio set my sights on another girl in his office: a blonde, with marvelous mammaries and, as he put it, only slightly smarter than a spicy Camps Bay samosa.

Silvio later became my best man – never a more suited term for the guy who'd reluctantly introduced me to the woman who would alter my life forever. And for the better. Sadly, Silvio is gone, leaving behind two delightful daughters and a wonderful wife: Audrey possesses a temperament that could put up with Silvio, and a spirit that is very much in line with that of Bridget.

The thing I loved about Bridget from the very start was that she was the first woman I could just be with who seemed to be okay with the notion that I could drop dead tomorrow or catch the next plane. Her plan, her life, her dreams would go forward without a glitch. She didn't play up to me or try to grab onto me emotionally. Bridget was perfectly content to sit alongside me at the beach, as we browned like berries and read without saying a word for hours on end. When she did speak, it was always good thoughts, and almost taunting me with the notion that I could come or go. No problem. Bridget Willis was apparently enjoying my company but it was for her only a temporary condition. I was a pleasant distraction.

Undaunted, I escalated my efforts, and told bold-faced lies to her about my time in uniform, my family wealth, my overnight successes and conquests, all of which were simply water off her smoothly tanned back. I even bought Bridget a book, *Ethan Frome,* an unrequited and tragic love story. I inscribed it for her. I thought that it would pierce her emotional shell-casing. It was to no avail. I even stooped to flirting openly with the gorgeous costumed and well-cleavaged waitresses at Whatley's Girls over monkey-gland steaks. Bridget remained openly unimpressed. She was the yin to my egotistical yang and had her own plan, in which I was only a brief, and perhaps even playful, pastime.

I think Freud said it, using medical terms, but I could be mistaken: men light up like a blast furnace, red hot in a flash and then stone cold again within the snap of your fingers. Women, on the other hand, warm up over time, simmering slowly. Like a dormant volcano, it takes a good woman longer, but once the lid is off … stand back. In my head, I was a Don Juan: an impostor counting notches in my boxer shorts. Bridget was the first woman I saw myself trying to breathe alongside for the rest of my life.

I'd never encountered a more immovable female before, and seemingly without effort this Willis woman had me totally and fully addicted. After laying on layers of false bravado, the light bulb was illuminated: I could just be myself with Bridget, and she appeared to want very little to do with me.

When I left her, and Cape Town, I was saddened to think it would be the last time we'd be together, a feeling I'd had during adolescence when I'd spend hours on the phone with a girlfriend, only to miss her the moment I hung up the receiver. When I arrived at the office in Johannesburg, there was a beautifully wrapped coffee-table book of Africana awaiting me, with no return address. Inside the front cover was a note from Bridget, which said, 'I do love you too, but I just didn't know how to say it. B.'

Like in the movie – 'We got Annie!'

To this day, I don't think even Bridget knew the scheming, conniving and covert overtures I made to get her to pick me. When we sold the TrekAmerica business to the company that was Bridget's South African employer, I had an ace card to play. The founder of TrekAmerica, 'JJ', wanted to take his money off the table and vanish posthaste, leaving behind a management team that appeared ready to implode. I too put my hand up to say I'd be leaving the building, and the new owners asked what it might take to have me linger a bit longer and facilitate a smooth transition. More money was no motivation, and I hinted that I was more than keen on spending time around Bridget. The new owners suggested an offer that was too tough to turn down: they gave me carte blanche to pick my team, which could include making an offer to 'transfer Bridget *if she liked'*, to the USA to help out. I signed up on the spot. And I applied my best sales pitch to Bridget to please, pretty-please, join me in America. I promised fun and adventure and heaps of other incentives. Bridget said yes, she'd come along for the ride.

A month after the sale, the rest of the longstanding management team rioted over new contracts and dollars, threatening to walk off en masse. I refused to join the dissenting chorus. Instead I bought one-way tickets and Bridget and I lit out for Orlando, Florida. I made it clear to both sides of the negotiations that they should give me a call when they'd sorted themselves out. I had the deal I wanted and I was going to stay on.

I would call in every few days from Disney World or Epcot or Panama City or New Orleans, to learn who had resigned, who was staying on. I declined to leave a phone number where we could be reached. My fellow workmates repeatedly reprimanded and belittled me about how I'd abandoned the cause of my pals. The new overseas owners asked me to intervene on their behalf, or if I couldn't, then simply stay out of the line of fire and lay low until the fog over Trek's future lifted.

All of those comments fell firmly onto deaf Mickey Mouse ears. I was as happy as it gets. Bridget and I would feed the coin slot of the phone quarters to call her folks in Cape Town to say we were very, very happy and doing 'just fabulously fine'. All five of the other dissenters deserted, suggesting the company would crumble within a year.

Bridget and I happily moved into 'the manor' and set up house, alongside, at times, 20 other Trek tour leaders, shop staff and office help, depending on the season. We started our first joint bank account, lobbing $200 there, and bought a television set with a 22-inch screen and a remote control. We were more than 50-50 partners. Bridget would become my religion.

Game changer!

Bridget was the only female pal I ever introduced to my family. When I told my brother David I wanted to visit for a weekend with Bridget, I highlighted the notion that she was a keeper, but didn't want to create an awkward situation with his and Ellen's kids about nesting arrangements. We could, if they preferred, just visit for the day. My brother, keen to see me, said it would not be a problem, we were both welcome for as long as we cared to stay. Patrick and Meghan, alongside my brother and his wife, loved Bridget, making us both feel at home whenever we invaded.

In their kitchen one sunny August afternoon, Ellen asked Bridget what her immigration status was, and Bridget's matter-of-fact reply shocked me to my core; her visa was up in a month, and she figured she'd be heading back to Cape Town. I couldn't see me without her, and while stuck in traffic on the Belt Parkway, I asked her to please, pretty-please marry me. She said she might, if we could do it without heaps of fanfare, and I agreed. When we phoned her parents to say we were getting married, her dad, Captain Willis, asked only half-jokingly when the baby was 'due.'

In New York state, we could get a marriage license at the courthouse with the right paperwork, my brother David asked a judge who played bagpipes in the Hibernian band with him to do the honors in his chambers, and the following Friday, we snuck off early for a four-day 'weekend' to Long Island.

Bridget went shopping for a wedding dress and had her hair done, my beautiful brother set up a massive 10-man tent on the back lawn, equipped with lighting and a four-poster bed for the bridal suite, and for my bachelor's party my brother-in-law 'JO', David and I went to see the movie *Star Wars*! My brother-by-another-mother, Shane Boocock, came out on the day for the event. I was happy from top to bottom.

In December of that same year, we went to Cape Town where Bridget's folks and friends planned a wonderful church service, compete with a ribboned Rolls Royce – the car of a close friend – and a backyard banquet. Another fabulous day. I bought a new blue suit, and for the first time in years, sat down for a barber's haircut and a shave. My new bride had requested it.

Here I was, a confirmed bachelor, married *twice* in the same year!

I missed almost every anniversary afterwards, until I married the same gal for the third time, in Australia, only this time I had to sneak up on her and put her on the spot to get a 'yes' for our twentieth anniversary. It was a massive, successful and total conspiracy with our kids actively involved in the event.

Nest sites – we went looking!

Bridget and I were spoiled with choices. When we left Trek, we spent the better part of a year to select the next roost to nest in. We'd already made overtures in Sydney, Cape Town, New York and LA. Bridget was drawn to Charleston, South Carolina, where we had family, saying the city spoke to her. History, arts and culture, the must-have great beaches. All lures, topped off by the offer for her of a really well-paying job in corporate travel. We'd lived in Charleston for almost a year, happily when Cody arrived and changed our lives forever.

CHAPTER 5

Travel with Our Trio and Merrily Toting Tiny-Tons More Luggage!

Historically, when I'm confronted with hard-to-deal-with issues, I simply run! It's hard to hit a moving target. When our deal for the handover and sale of Trek to the new lads from Trek America was completed, the new owners kept me on as window dressing to roll out at major travel shows and expos. I loved doing these consulting director's jaunts, as for a brief time I would be back in front of old travel and trekking pals and peers. As a dormant director, they continued to engage me in the business and update me on the travel scene while adding dollars to the Cody coffers.

At one of these events, the new ownership of Trek took me aside and asked me to do a series of major launches alongside Insight Vacations, the newly appointed general sales agents (GSA) for TrekAmerica, in Australia, New Zealand, Asia and South Africa. I balked, politely begging off as the assignment was for three-plus months in the Pacific. I mentioned that Bridget and I were trying to make a nest in Charleston, and that we had a newly landed son to look after. The offer they made was seductive, and intentionally included taking both Bridget and Cody along for the ride at the company's expense. My toe started tapping.

What I didn't learn until later, was that the deal I'd set up a few years earlier for TrekAmerica at Insight Vacations was seriously about to come undone *unless* they got the Sheehans back to help with the new blitz campaign. Insight's managing director Chris Newman made it clear: No Sheehans, no general sales agents for South Africa, Asia, Malaysia, New Zealand and Australia. It's very nice to be wanted.

Global nomad! Or just plain mad?!

When it was just we three, Bridget, Cody and me, we were literally all over the map. I was offered another sweetheart consulting assignment, lasting a wee bit over a year, which would put money in our coffers, pay our way for nearly everything, and we'd be able to collect rent money on our newly renovated place in Charleston. I jumped enthusiastically at the notion, while beautiful Bridget reminded me that it was not a duet we were dealing with any longer, but there were three to please. Previously, we would bob and weave, elect short-term assignments in far outpostings with great abandon, but we didn't have babies, medications, special dietary needs, or other items like nebulizers for Cody's cystic fibrosis, play pens, toys and let us not forget, baby blankets.

Apparently, my would-be employers held my ability to sell travel, launch new products or break into new markets (or snake-oil elixirs) in very high regard, and agreed to fund better bed allowances, airfares for three and other family-oriented concessions to my payroll package. So we plunged ahead, with me on the front line for the campaign, while Bridget stayed firmly focused with the single-minded purpose of looking after kid-Cody.

Have Cody will travel ... and travel!

When I presented Bridget with the prospects of lighting out for Australia for a month consulting assignment, I thought I'd have to do some fancy snake-oil sales pitch. Even then, I put my odds at less than 50-50. I was wrong again. Bridget said going along would pose special challenges for us as a family, but if it was what I really wanted, we'd somehow make it work. Yes! We planned in advance, Bridget sorted out the paperwork and necessities of toting a tot halfway around the world, and then being able to tap into the best medical help available. She did this all long before we owned our first home computer, and there were no apps or internet zips, or anything that circumvented the old-fashioned way of digging, reading, calling, sending telexes, and racing to the post office to send a fax down the line. My mobile phone weighed in at two kilos and was the size of a military walkie-talkie. Australia here we come! With New Zealand tossed in on the side as a nearby appetizer.

An adventure! Let's just go for, say, three months, shall we?

For over three months, Bridget and Cody-son were side by side and inseparable. I'd dart in and out of our temporary home base, while Bridget held court and the fort in every major Australian city. We had a handsome budget and expense account and Bridget used it to full advantage. Cody beamed with every new venue, and our system worked wonderfully. I was running away, yet again, but this time I had good company.

This notion that as a family we could still travel with kids in tow, added a new, pleasing dimension (not detention!) to being 'married with kids'. If having kids, or children with 'special needs' was meant to inhibit travel, somebody thankfully forgot to tell Bridget!

In every new location, Bridget would seek out local medical practitioners, make visits with Cody for review, and join in local events that could engage our son with other kids. Bridget had childhood friends and relationships from her adventures with Encounter Overland and from other travel she'd done long before we met, so she re-found friends in every host city.

February 1990, Mandela Vry!

> Tomorrow, Nelson Mandala is to be free after 27 years
> in prison. Cody's just turned one here in Cape Town and
> the undertones of our being in South Africa for Mandela's
> release scare me. Silvio, my 'best man' and I have
> made plans to take our families up the touristy cable

car attraction to the top of Table Mountain. It overlooks all of Cape Town and the view is spectacular on a clear day. Bridget and Audrey, Silvio's wife, wanted us instead to take our kids (they have two beautiful daughters) to Greenmarket Square for the historic event, a notion we husbands have flatly refused. Instead, I've discreetly packed my tote with enough of Cody's meds, a dozen jars of applesauce and dried biltong to last an entire week. I've also got my Buck knife – a gift from my kid brother Chris – and binoculars so I can monitor from a distance the tempo of the predominantly black crowd when Mandela addresses an audience after 27 years in prison.

Yesterday I earmarked a sailboat in the harbor to commandeer if we need to evacuate the country. The undercurrent was that if things got ugly it'd go from bad to bloody faster than a runaway train. I'm a pretty good sailor. Silvio is also covertly laden with food stuffs and the plastic first aid kit from the glovebox of his VW Kombi. I've always been a worry wart.

– Journal entry, Cape Town, South Africa,
10 February 1990

Outhouse vs whorehouse? Take your pick!

Bridget was nothing short of brilliant when it came to researching and booking our family-friendly accommodations everywhere we went. With the exception of one rare occasion when I stepped up to the plate, using my significant connections to make our Melbourne living arrangements. I now know better than to step in, putting my foot in where it simply doesn't belong: up my butt.

Part of our Australian assignment was to spend a total of eight weeks in Victoria, with our anchor dropped in the city of Melbourne. Fabulous, as it's a city with great outdoors, wonderful eateries, museums, shopping and entertainment. I had a contact who looked after multiple properties and made significant boasts about our accommodation: 'Leave it with me, Mark! I've got a great, fully furnished two-bedroom palace in the heart of the action, close to everything … you'll absolutely adore it!' I gave it the thumbs-up without looking at his recommendation, suggesting to my wife it was going to be simply astounding.

We arrived on a blistering hot Friday afternoon, after an intersection-choked stop-and-go drive to collect the keys. We were all exhausted, and very ready to settle into our 'palace of a place' in the vibrant heart of St Kilda.

Parking on the main drag proved to be problematic, highlighted by the fact that a drunken local had stretched across my parking place, demanding a donation to vacate the space. Already alarms were beginning to go off. I could tell by the look in my wife's eye (I could only see one at the time, as I casually tried to reposition the drunk) that she was having significant doubts of her own.

When the manager unlocked the chipped door to our new abode, I advised Bridget, who was holding our barefooted son, that under no circumstances was she to put him down on the rug (I assumed at one time it was a light gray, now matured into a crap-brown and boasting a shellac-like coating of slime-mold). The place smelled like human manure. Our 'palace' was nothing short of a shithole, and I could see the divorce papers being fast-tracked by Bridget for overnight delivery. This was truly my doing. It didn't require a gypsy fortune teller or a crystal ball to determine I was falling well short of success with my spouse.

Out in the car again, while waiting for the drunk, who'd bent the radio antenna on our bonnet backwards, to be hoisted into a police wagon, we studied our options. I was going to just throw money at a sweet suite in a five-star inner-city hotel until we could find something and, while driving, Bridget spotted a sign for long-term executive homes. I called the billboard number and got a South African female's voice on the phone. A blessing in disguise, when I asked her to save my family and my marriage she said, sadly, she had nothing wonderful until the coming Monday.

Home sweet home – to the happy hooker!

Then, after a pause she said, wait up, I *can* put you into a four-bedroom townhouse in a great location with a yard, but it will only be for two nights if that'll preserve your relationship! I promised to name my next offspring after her and took the place sight unseen.

It was spectacular: a white-washed three-story Greek-style home, in fashionable Toorak, with off-street parking and all the creature comforts. We settled in well, and while I was patting myself on the back, we over-ordered takeaway food. While waiting for the delivery kid's finger on the front garden buzzer, the phone started to ring off the hook.

I answered it the first few times, and each male caller wanted to know when they might call around to see Shelia. I suggested they had the wrong number and hung up. Then, while I was out at the gate tipping the delivery kid, Bridget answered: the male caller asked off the cuff if she did oral or anal. He wanted to know in advance before he and his buddy jumped into a taxi from the city. He hinted money was no object if she'd take it up the butt without lubrication.

For the next five calls, Bridget did a bit of seductive interrogation and discovered the contracted housekeeper, knowing the place was intended to be empty for the entire weekend, had placed an advert for whoring at our address. After all, the place was meant to be empty till Monday.

We eventually took the phone off the hook and advised the agency of our discovery. The firm, severely embarrassed, charged us nothing for the two-night stay, and I adopted the dulcet tones of an undercover vice officer when men rocked up to hit the buzzer at all hours of the evening while we were there.

Bridget has a way of making the best of the seemingly worst situation and we could have laughed through the entire event, with one sizzling exception. While in our whorehouse abode, Cody took a fancy to a modern light fixture which featured an exposed and flickering light bulb. It resembled the lure of a glowing fire, and in fact, after it had been illuminated for a few hours, became furnace hot. Kid Cody, being naturally curious, grabbed it. It is hard enough on a kid when he's got CF, but when you add a scalding burn to the mixture it makes matters much worse. Cody kept up a constant, all-night vigil of tears, and I knew, in my heart of hearts, it was *all* my fault.

'We're very, very sorry! Did we say *sorry* yet?'

The best part of the bedding disaster was the booking agency, in an attempt to quell my rage, offered us a three-bedroom garden apartment in Toorak. It was the private residence of a corporate giant of industry, with private underground parking, rare oil paintings on the walls and antiques everywhere. The place was far beyond fabulous.

That weekend, I bought Cody his very first car. It was a gloss-white battery-powered BMW, and with the 'pedal to the metal' could muster up to 8 miles (13 kilometres) per hour. It ran for two hours non-stop without recharging. Bridget was sure I'd lost my mind, perhaps due to sleep deprivation, but Cody loved that car and drove it from room to room in our executive setting, occasionally pinging into high-priced Queen Anne antiques, or making a full circle chasing me around the kitchen, patio area and living room. Even though we didn't have room, that car, with care, got toted across every Australian state except for Tasmania. Cody loved it, and he was always pleased to share it with his cousins whenever we connected. Sometimes the thing had to carry three kids stacked on it like layered pancakes, which dropped its top speed to about two clicks an hour. Got a problem? Throw more powerful batteries at it!

Home *is* where the heart is

I've been away in regional Victoria for the past five days, leaving Bridget and Cody carless. Nothing slows this duo down; they took the Melbourne tram everywhere, got library cards and signed up for weekly playtime classes. Bridge hired movies and decorated the new place with kid art everywhere. Blu Tack was a constant tenant in Bridget's bags and kid artworks even made an appearance in the en suite toilet where our Cody was learning to linger on the plastic 'loo'.

Bridget had connected with a Cape Town classmate from her boarding-school days who has a son Cody's age and they spent serious time gallivanting about. Photos with Santa and the elves, carols in the park and picnics at the local playgrounds. Tomorrow we're booked to board the 'Puffing Billy' train where we get to dangle our feet out the windows in the open carriages as we fly through Victorian countryside at a breathtaking 7 miles [12 kilometres] an hour, which is why the one-way trip to the historic gold town restoration takes an hour to accomplish. Bridget takes fabulous photos, toting her camera alongside all the other gear she needs for Cody-kid. I'm happier than I can recall in this duo's company. MY family …

– Journal entry, Dandenong Ranges, Victoria, 1990

Gallivanting around

Because I was involved in travel, even when our family grew to include Dylan and Hayley, we were able to gallivant around on occasion with the entire family in tow. Being well-connected in tourism and travel offered opportunities that might have been costly otherwise. I'd plan my 'hotel inspection' trips to coincide with school holidays, or brief lapses in Cody's need for internment at the hospital. Hotels, attractions, tour operators, airline partners and eateries were happy to host us, and we usually got the sweetest of suites while I was working.

On the road again

I come from a family that spent every summer of my kid-hood packing and unpacking the family station wagon. My older brothers Robert and David, alongside our father, would lay everything we needed for a summer at the beach in Rocky Point, Long Island out on the driveway and then they'd monkey around with all the gear, packing and unpacking while still leaving sufficient room inside the cabin for the six kids, two adults, assorted pets, strollers and a collapsible baby's crib. I spent the entire journey one year laying prone in a military belly-crawl posture alongside my kid sister Cathy, with whom I fought like cats and dogs, and on the other side a ripe-smelling and much-loved Boxer dog name Ginger. We made frequent roadside stops for my small bladder, while topping up the water in the goldfish bowls.

Any parent who travels with kids in tow knows it: the journey is almost always monumental and memorable, and you never forget what it took to get out the front door. With Cody, as with any other special needs child aboard, there are a few necessities that simply can't be left behind on the kitchen counter or forgotten when exiting the last hotel or resort for the long, lone road to the Grand Canyon.

I once left our son Dylan's blanket (aka 'Blankee') in a resort hotel and I was for years afterwards plagued with the guilt. Multiple calls and threats to 'find it' to the hotel, the hotel, assisted by a large reward offered, failed to locate Blankee, and an impostor blanket was spotted immediately by our son. Even Cody cried out, 'Dad, that's not Dylan's blanket!'

With a cystic fibrosis kid around, no amount of toy offers or amusement park passes do the trick. You can't 'make it up' if you leave off the stuff your child needs to keep him or her breathing or eating. And over half the stuff you need for a CF child requires a battery of batteries, electrical gizmos and connections which send every airport security officer into rapid red alert. The remarkable new nebulizer medicines all seem to demand non-stop-refrigeration. And all of this vital inventory has to travel on board with mom and dad, in the event that the checked luggage arrives in Chicago while the family is alighting in New York.

I should get Bridget to write this portion, as about 50 per cent of Cody's earlier sojourns were made with his mom while I'd already left the scene days earlier for work. I've seen it in action with other families on the move. With each change of position, kids and parents do a visual inventory to confirm they still have the right number of offspring, the right number of rolling bags, backpacks, teddy bears, bottles, blankets and baseball caps. Nobody ever intends to drop a baby; yet it happens every day.

'Are those your underpants on the conveyor?!'

I sent out an all-points bulletin a few years back for a book I was doing entitled 'Are Those Your Underpants on the Conveyor?!', a collection of trip-over-your-own-toes travel bloopers. I asked for contributions from every point of the compass, friends and family from all over the globe. The odd thing was that even the busiest people I knew took the time to write something for the campaign: Richard Branson, John Cleese, Vivienne Westwood, Michael Palin, Bryce Courtney, Kamahl, Bill Bryson … each took the time to chip-in. My intention was to flex a fundraising muscle and use the book's royalties as a funny, positive way of finding a CF cure. What I got back by the bushel-full of funny stuff was more than enough bloopers to fill 15 books. Even today I get unsolicited stories on this topic. Maybe the next book could be entitled 'Are those Your Knickers on the …?' The thing I took away from all of it was: If you only ask, you at very least, have the potential of success. Don't ask, don't get. Good people really did want to help but they are flat-out busy. Sometimes it takes a kid like Cody to come along and ask what's possible.

Oops! I Bad! It happens …

I still recall with small waves of shock, arriving already puffed to the family's miles-off boarding gate when my wonderful wife asked me to confirm the whereabouts of Cody's must-have nebulizer. I could readily confirm that it was still safe, back in the security checkpoint miles behind me, awaiting my collection! I hold a high school track record in my hometown of Manhasset for the 120-yard low hurdles, but I'm pretty sure I would have broken the record for tearing through duty free shops as smiling assistants sprayed me as I sprinted past, with the latest in Polo cologne.

When the airline hostess assigned to helping families with small children to board suggested that we might have to off-load the troops and wait for the following day's flight, I advised Bridget to board and strap the kids in. I'd be 'right back'.

'Sorry sir, that might not be possible as we're intending to close the gate and secure the aircraft for an on-time departure.'

I can be faster than a speeding bullet when my adrenaline is aroused, and the prospect of losing a wife and kids in the process is at stake! I didn't start breathing properly until we were at 35,000 feet and Captain Probert took off the fasten seatbelts sign. Beautiful Bridget, who was anchored with the kids calmly across the aisle, was, I'm sure, contemplating divorce, as the nebulizer was the *only thing*, I was meant to guard with every single pore I possessed (all of which, were still wide open and sweating buckets of perspiration). Thankfully the seat next to me was unoccupied. I took myself off to the toilet and engineered in the small cubicle an 'English shower' using about a zillion paper towels to dry myself.

Balancing the books

I've always fretted about money, even when we seemed to have more than enough of it. When Bridget agreed to take over our checkbook, and the painful paying of bills, I welcomed this offer with open arms. It, for me, was freedom; all I needed to do was make the money, and my life partner, my Bridget, would see to the spending of it for the common good. We never talked about how much we had (or didn't!) and that suited me as fine as a Stradivarius fiddle for years.

I never asked, and Bridget never offered updates, except to ask what was possible. Could we plan to take the family to Africa for a Namibian adventure? Or fund a family reunion in the Hawaiian Island for 50? Or the new, not yet FDA-approved CF drug which showed great prospects for our son? We were hand in glove on all of it, and I merrily bounded ahead to add to the clan's coffers.

Picking priorities; staying on the track

As a kid, when I found myself at the top of a wobbling pine, wind whipping the tip, precariously perched up there, it was too late to reconsider my options. I had only three choices that appeared to me: I could stay up there until the fates conspired to provide me a way out, I could struggle in fear back the way I came, to the bastards on the ground, bigger kids who were intend on killing me, or I could simply jump. I've been jumping my entire life, hoping the branches I encountered on the way down would break my fall. Oddly enough, the kids on the ground figured I was totally insane, turned tail and ran. Being a parent, there is no easy way down.

– Note in a bottle

Seize the day

Bridget, more than once a month, made the comment that we should not put life on hold when we had the opportunity to try something new, or invest in our children. It got so she never even had to say it any longer; we just adopted this notion into our lifestyle. We'd travel when we were able, fully enjoy the places we went, and would invest heavily in the best schools for all our kids, 'even if it means we'll have to work harder, or longer later'. She was right. We plowed money and love, energy and care into our kids, and got back heaps of good things in return. At times, we spent money like candy on the road, to watch our pennies when we unpacked our suitcases. Cody's motto, cut into his shoulder in Latin as a CF adult, translates to 'seize the day'. And although I detest tattoos, I must say he picked a good one.

'Let's try and make the most of this, for as long as we can. Travel widely, educate the kids, and connect with our families and friends. There's no time to store up rainy days or wait around for leisurely retirement. I don't mind, if you and I have to go back to work at 60, let's grab what we've got in front of us right now.'

CHAPTER 6

Family Matters |

My family is a bit like mercury

In the 7th grade, I had the best ever teacher in science, and although he appeared to be a bit absentminded, he opened countless numbers of punk kids' heads to things they didn't have a clue about before they landed their ass in his classroom chairs. Mr Leake wore red socks, or no socks at all, and sometimes he even wore a pair of socks that were in no way related to each other in fabric, design or color.

One day he left a vial of mercury out on the formica-topped table unattended, and I swiped it to take to my roost at the back of the class. I could roll it out into my palm, shinier than silver, and it would hold its most unusual shape. When I separated it with my free wooden Wright Hardware ruler, it would re-form itself into an exact replica of the larger portion. I could do this as many times as I pleased. It was like splitting atoms in the palm of my hand. When I reintroduced the independent pieces to each other, they presented again in the exact same shape as before. Pure magic. This is how I view my nuclear family; the people I love, and I know for certain love me.

We separate, we go through changes and yet, whenever we are emotionally or physically reconnected, we form one very shiny, even magical potion. Like mercury, our family possesses some of the most remarkable properties. Mercury poisoning is also possible if you are exposed to too much of it ...

It's as easy as riding a bike, right?

I seemed always to be short of breath as a kid. Which went a long way to explaining why my kid sister always got the silver dollars our dad handed over to the kid who could lap an entire city block on Hudson River Drive in New York fastest. I could beat anyone on a short sprint, but on any long haul, I ran out of puff before we made the first corner. My sister Cathy had much better lungs, so I think maybe that's the reason I enjoyed tormenting her, a dangerous proposition as she was our father's repeatedly proclaimed 'Princess'. As a very skinny kid, it took me over a week to learn how to ride a bike, while my smart kid-sister Cathy, triumphantly soloed the two-wheeler during her very first attempt. This prompted me to direct her into a summer-time hedgerow, loaded with red-trimmed poison ivy bushes. She either had to run me over or divert into the poisonous patch. At family gatherings to this day, Cathy still recounts the story of the poison ivy.

That very same week of the bike, I busted the windows

out of our neighbor's chicken coop in Rocky Point. And I got caught with the rocks in my pockets. My mother defended my terrorist tendencies, saying I was hyperactive and that was the reason I was always as skinny as an ironing board. I was a total jitterbug as a kid, who was never able to gain weight. I couldn't hold my breath underwater for long, but I could fidget even while sleeping upright. Mr St Andrew, the owner of the broken glass, flatly refused to take money for reparations, instead insisting that I help him build a tall wall between our properties to keep me out. Mr St Andrew taught me how to mix concrete, how to lay a dozen bricks in under a minute and how to keep a wheelbarrow headed in a straight line. He gave me a $10 bill when we were finished and told our mother she was absolutely right about my seemingly endless amount of pent-up energy. The wall never kept me away, and I helped build the wall on the other side of the house, spread gravel onto the driveway, and cut down and tote a rotting front-yard tree. We had no inkling then that I was toting around the sleeping, cystic fibrosis gene.

I wasn't always a nice kid, but I always knew I was going to grow up okay and emulate my heroes like 'honest' Abe Lincoln, Martin Luther King Jr and President John F. Kennedy. My pals all wanted to be astronauts, or firemen, or cops. My iconic older brother Bobby wanted to be a G-man, and my best friend, my brother David, wanted to be a priest. Cathy wanted to be a veterinarian, or a schoolteacher and my other sister wanted to be a nurse. Our parents raised us with one voice, to be good, solid adults, and even when I occasionally went outside the bounds, they were always there for me. They used the glue of love to keep my siblings and me on track. And they had us all convinced we could be anything we wanted to be – if we wanted it badly enough.

Losing our Christopher

Losing my kid brother Chris was a real shock, as I always assumed the youngest of the Sheehans was bulletproof. In the end, and at his request I spent the last eight weeks of his life alongside him in Brisbane, so he could die at home. Beautiful Bridget, my sisters Cathy and Anne, along with our kids flew up often to visit, and Chris's sons came daily, calling first to be sure he'd be at his best for the gathering. Chris didn't want his two wonderful sons and their partners to have to change bedpans, hoist him or care for him constantly. When the doctors said nothing was working and recommended a hospice Chris pleaded to die at home.

I'm a walking advertisement for the folks of palliative care, who came every single day, helped me with his morphine and meds, installed a full-on hospital bed, wheelchairs and more for his final run. I was grateful to have that time with Chris, as we shared childhood good times again, rang up old buddies from our hometown and spoke for hours on end. I took the occasional run to the bottle shop for his beloved $8 bottle of wine. He and I had made a pact years earlier when our mother died, which we both honored to the end. How often do you get the chance to have such a meaningful farewell?

In the end it was not the grog (Chris referred to himself, most of the time, as a functional alcoholic), or cigarettes, or pot, or prescriptions that killed him, and I'd never-ever, wish asbestos cancer on even my worst enemy.

Like the dirt under childhood fingernails, it got into his lungs

There were six really good blokes in his team, as they water-blasted the innards of Australian navy ships that were being decommissioned. Every pipe and overhead beam, every boiler or tank was gift-wrapped in tiny, unseen barbs that lodged themselves in my kid brother's lungs. All of the crew wore top-to-bottom safety gear and breathers but the small, fatal needlepoints floated in the air for days afterwards.

Exit strategy – too tired to fight

On his final Sunday, my two sisters flew in, and the doc discreetly gave me an adrenaline boost of some type (I was injecting him 4–5 times a day with powerful painkillers) and Chris, surrounded by his loved ones, faked enjoying a cheeseburger (he'd stopped eating and drinking two days earlier) for our benefit: my sister Cathy commented he was looking the best she'd seen him in months. And then, when everyone was gone, I lifted him into his bed for the last time ... he stopped breathing on three occasions for many minutes and then, suddenly, revived. When I whispered to him it was okay to let go, he still hung on. I phoned his sons, who came to the bedside, held him tight, and then, only then, was he willing to let go. I'm still reeling.

Years earlier, Christopher flew in from Australia and was there in Philadelphia on the night our mother died. When the nurse gave my mother the pills she needed to keep breathing, she called me near, and discreetly spat the tablets into my palm. She'd had enough. Chris, saw me pocket the pills, the only witness to this, and said nothing. He sat with her for hours, holding her hand. I fell asleep in a bedside chair, and maybe an hour later he woke me to say 'Look, Mom's awake.' Her eyes were wide open, and she was gone.

Chris left his mark and marker on everyone he ever met: he gifted me with tool sets, chainsaws, lawnmowers, and more. He loved machines, even as a little kid, and every day around the house I see his hen scratches on things.

Family treasure buried in a massive blue bank vault

It took me and his two sons a full day to move his bank-sized-safe from its anchor, where he'd left us clues on how to open it scrawled on the door. When we finally got the vault door opened, his most valued possessions sprawled out onto the driveway like a peacock's feathers.

There for safekeeping were hundreds of family photos, a collection of silver dollars our father gifted us each for birthdays and a few of his most-loved tools. Two envelopes tucked at the back each contained babyteeth from his boys that he'd locked away after swiping them from the tooth fairy. I've not wept that way in years.

> Kid-brother Chris gifted us with another set of ratchet wrenches this morning and put a chunky red brick in the cistern of my toilet. The brick, did not have the name SHEEHAN printed on it, as did the hundreds of other items he's generously come laden with to visit our front door. I think Chris figured nobody would want to swipe

a wet brick. The purpose of the brick, as he explained to Cody and me, was to by 'displacement' reduce our consumption of water every time we flushed the bog. There is drought on here, and water use is restricted.

– Journal entry

Day won/one!

I'm almost afraid to say the good stuff, for fear of jinxing it all, or temping the fates.

Ben and Tim visited, bringing a box of things from Chris shortly after he died. Among the items was a Brooks Brothers shirt I *knew* was his favorite – bought with me at the big brands discount mall in Hawaii. I wore it to a function with Cody at the US Consul General's residence, and I seemed to walk a few inches taller, and felt a few pounds lighter, and a whole lot of my insides warmer. I had this elated feeling I'd not had in ages: my son doing well, my family settled and strong, and I had the notion that everything was right with the world. Some things change with the snap of your fingers, while others take longer to seep into your pores, and on very rare occasions everything that's good, and sound and wonderful with the world reaches me.

'Dad, you look as if you've been crying.' No son, I'm just not used to the light air up here.

Cody's multiple mothers!

Cody is very proud to have multiple mothers. He knows he's been overly blessed with his mom, but the fact is there are a fair few others who can, and have stepped up to play the role from the time he needed a nappy change until now decades later. I agree with him, they're all candidates for cloning.

His Aunt Cathy will drive hours back and forth and has donned her PJs and slept on a hospital cot when Cody was a kid and incarcerated for weeks at a time. She'd tote her own daughters along with mountains of materials to build 'stuff' on the hospital ward with Cody and his other ward pals. I think part of her bad lower-back issues stem from her sitting on those tiny wooden kid chairs for hours helping other hospital-bound kids cope with the challenges of making cardboard masks and paper Christmas decorations for the ward.

His Aunt Anne, and her husband Jim Olsen were there the night Cody was born and filled in just fine for me when some time later, Bridget was having Dylan while I was 9000 miles (15,000 kilometres) off in Australia. She did all the things I would have done: run red lights, honk the horn non-stop and whisk Bridget off to the Charleston Hospital.

My sister, Anne made a dramatic shift after Jim's death, and moved lock, stock and great knitting skills to Sydney, and Cody enjoys fireside chats with his Auntie Anne on a weekly basis.

CHAPTER 7

Super Siblings! |

Once I got a feel for being a father, I started nudging for more kids. Cody-kid was such a bright spark for us, despite his CF, that I figured we should plan on a pal or two down the path. Coming from a family of six siblings, I didn't want Cody to be an only child and I began a quiet, frisky campaign, lobbying with Bridget to come to bed.

Knowing that there was a one-in-four chance our next child could also have cystic fibrosis was an emotional mind-twisting element to enlarging our family. Another CF parent I'd been corresponding with suggested that it was nothing short of playing a tabletop version of genetic Russian roulette. With a one-in-four chance of there being a loaded round in my pistol's chamber. My penpal knew what she was talking about; years earlier, she'd had a second child with CF before testing was readily available. She'd outlived both her CF children when she started to write to me. There are families who have two or three children with CF. I can't imagine how tough that might be, especially if you apply the more recent theory that all CF sufferers need to be at least five feet apart at all times. Bridget wanted more family as well, but we would have to do testing through the early stages of pregnancy.

Mixed emotions – I mixed more drinks; Bridget gave up grog altogether!

When Bridget announced that we were pregnant for the second time I had mixed emotions while we waited on an emotional ledge for the test results. I wanted to leap with joy for both of us but feared what might happen if the test results came back with CF and sadness attached to them. In all other aspects 'within her control' Bridget had it covered. She gave up alcohol, avoided smoke-filled social events and continued to eat intelligently and attend regular medical check-ups. Bridget was never anything other than a one or two glass social wine sipper. I made up for her abstaining, elevating my under-the-table drinking.

Dylan Thomas

Our Dylan arrived two weeks early in Charleston, sabotaging my intention to be home with ample time to cut the umbilical cord that connected him to his mom. Bridget said that Dylan did kick a lot while he was in there! On the day Dylan Thomas was born in Charleston, in the very same birthing suite as his brother, I was in my sister's home on the Port Hacking River in Sydney's south. Dylan, I can only guess, was eager for air of his own, but I did manage to stay on the phone line long enough to hear his vocal cords, keen for attention. Tears at my end.

I was receiving updates by phone and taking champagne in advance of the event with my sister Cathy and her family when I got the phone call. I'm pretty sure we'd have named Dylan differently, but Bridget deferred because I was unable to be there for the opening ribbon-cutting ceremony. I've taken flack over the years for introducing Cody's bestest buddy as 'Dylan Thomas' but I always felt the necessity of separating this wonderful person from the other Dylans who got named because of the then-popular heartthrob actor from the Beverly Hills postcode TV program.

I didn't even have a chance to drop my bag when I landed in Charleston before Cody was beaming. My Cody appeared to be rapidly fan-drying his hands like a Charleston flapper. It was pure adrenaline in action. Cody had a fabulous baby brother: 'Dad, Dad, he's named Dylan, me and Mom named him. Dad, and oh my gosh Dad (the words now melding together like one), he's great! Dad, Dad! He smiles at everything, and Mom lets me hold him! Don't worry, she showed me how and I'm careful!'

During the entire introduction to my new son by our Cody, his hands fanned with excitement. I was feeling the very same way, flapping on the inside. Cody had a pal for life, and I cradled them both in my arms, Cody holding his kid brother, me holding them both. Bridget, across the room, would have been the only one to see that I was crying.

Dylan Thomas was cute from the very start. And it was not just his parents who thought so. He'll tuck his head in today when he reads these words, but nothing much has changed from when he was an adorable, fun-loving kid. People like to follow Dylan, even if he has no aspirations to lead anyone anywhere. It's only one of the things that endears him to many. His love and loyalty towards his brother and sister are monumental, and I've witnessed in him a selfless determination to look after his siblings. Even from the perch of a middle child he continues to support, defend and protect with a passion the ones he loves.

> While packing to move from Hollywood Lane this morning, I found a tiny slide box: the kind you keep wooden matches in. When I slid it open, it revealed the tiniest tooth, along with a small envelope, folded and crunched. On the envelope was a child's rendering of a ten-dollar bill. The note in hen-scratch from Dylan read. 'Deer tothferry (DAD) please lev 10 for this one.itz wuthit.'

The dynamic duo! Cody's best pal, ever

I have the picture of Cody holding his new baby brother embedded in my memory. They say that if you have a flashback just before you leave the planet one image appears. I think the smile on Cody's face, looking up at his mother and father while cradling his new kid-brother Dylan will be mine. Cody has always been a happy kid. When his brother Dylan Thomas came along, he got even happier.

Our homes have always had sufficient bedrooms for the boys to be on their own, yet they lobbied with one voice to be bunk mates until they entered their teens. When we designed and built our own Hebel home on Peppercorn Ridge in Australia, our sons agreed to put a door between them and share a dual-basin bathroom.

> *'The greatest gift Mom and Dad ever gave us was each other.'*

– Kid-brother Christopher

I knew exactly how our sons felt; during my entire kidhood I was blessed with a best-buddy roommate – either David, or Robert, or Christopher. Like Cody and Dylan, in my younger years our clan shuffled homes like some folk shuffle cards. Even if our schools or town changed names, it was reassuring to constantly have my very best buddies come along for the ride.

In my father's heyday of corporate transfers, my very smart sister Cathy, who is exceptional with sums, 'did the math' and reported her findings: we'd attended 11 different schools in 8 years of chasing the scent of a dollar with our dad. Our mother never faltered once; as long as her kids were happy, she was happier.

A cross between Pooh Bear and the Hulk

Cody and his brother Dylan are as tight as any two siblings could ever hope to get. Blood brothers.

The thing about Dylan's devotion to his siblings has always been curious. He's either Ironman melded-into the Hulk, or he melts like soft butter when it comes to his brother and sister. I watched Dylan march casually in our front door with one of his bones protruding through shredded pants after falling off his skateboard. He had a nice gouge cut over his right eye as well, in case I was curious about his gray matter. His 'take' on his dripping-red medical condition could be described as apologetic casual: 'Dad, I think I messed up a bit!' Bowen, one of his buddies, had been towing Dylan Thomas behind the bike on a rope tightly secured at the waist when he encountered a crack in the pavement with his face. 'Dad, do you think it needs stitches?' Cool Hand Luke.

This very same fella, if witness to any aggression or potential pain inflicted on his brother or sister has two radically different reactions: on the one hand, when faced with overwhelming odds in the face of bullies, Dylan explodes in retaliation. He truly scares me. I feel for 'the other guy'. Yet, presented with a tiny blood-sample needle headed for his sibling's skin, Dylan simply passes out and takes to the floorboards.

On one occasion in the children's ward at Prince of Wales Hospital in Randwick, Dylan joined Cody and me at the nurses' station. Old-hat procedure for Cody, but the pretty young nurse was floundering to find a satisfactory vein for Cody's IV drip. One peek at the needle the nurse was intending to put into Cody's arm and Dylan discreetly settled down on the linoleum floor for a nap. The sight launched our Dylan-son straight into Neverland. I looked around and he was curled up like a puppy.

Yep! Yin and yang!

On the opposite side of Dylan's emotional picket fence, if you dare to mess with his siblings, kindly take cover as he morphs into a madman in their defense.

I once reluctantly watched from behind my coffee cup as Dylan confronted three much older boys who were bullying

Cody on the monkey bars in Lake Tahoe, California. Fists clenched and feet anchored he stood his ground against Cody's much larger teenaged tormentors. I was within earshot and resisted intervening to see how things might pan out. Dylan was clearly outnumbered and out-reached by the bullies. I held back, something very hard for me to do with my rage, as I watched the leader of this group, fists clenched, openly challenge Cody's kid brother.

Looking behind him for support, the largest bully of the bunch watched his two pals who were already in rapid retreat, and without daring to turn his back on Dylan, sheepishly backed off, abandoned the site. The notion that Dylan could have easily gotten his ass kicked never even occurred to him. Cody and Hayley are very lucky to have such a brother to share between them. Hail Dylan Thomas Sheehan!

A month later, I watched Cody confront serious odds in defense of his sister Hayley. For the second time in a month, I held back intervening. I was thinking that one day, I would not be within earshot of a crisis for my kids and able to step in to protect them from harm. A very sobering thought for a perpetual worry wart. I let this confrontation run its natural course. Cody-son stood his ground, Hayley hovered behind her brother for protection and the bully moved on to other prey. I mentally recorded the kid's features, hoping to run into him with a parent or two in tow; I've always wanted to tell a parent publicly if their kid's is a little shit.

Happy house mates, brotherly bedroom!

Cody and Dylan always shared a bedroom as tots, even when we had three of four bedrooms to spare. They insisted on it, liking each other's company, side-by-side beds, shared toys, synchronized Batman and Robin outfits, and the security blanket of having a protective brother nearby.

When we were planning our new home, the architect was dumbfounded by the notion that the boys would want the biggest bedroom in the new place and didn't mind bunking together. As the boys were getting older and we planned to live in our dream spot for years, we had to compromise and they reluctantly agreed to separate rooms, to take them well into their teens, while insisting on a shared bathroom.

When they did share, Cody's side of their bedroom was as neat as a pin, while Dylan's domain always looked as if a seasonal cyclone had recently made a visit; and yet they adored the proximity, each allowing for the other's space and freedom to choose. Dylan Thomas never noticed Cody was tidy and regimented in storing his things and Cody seemed oblivious to the mess across the carpet.

I admire this in them both. To this day Cody can be wearing cufflinks and pinstripes, dressed to the teeth, while Dylan looks like a remake of the 'Leaves of Grass' hippie, Walt Whitman. Tattered pants, more boxer shorts and ass showing than not; Cody in button-downs and highly glossed shoes; Dylan's stubbed toe sticking out of the end of his Vans skateboarding sneakers.

Princess Hayley invades 7000 feet above sea level

Hayley likes to tell people she was born in California, instead of spelling out the specifics of the town called Truckee where we actually cut the umbilical cord connecting her and her mom. Cody and Dylan loved their sister from the very moment they saw her; nothing's changed in all these years.

My daughter was born this morning, and I'm headed for Tahoe so I can collect our boys from school for a hospital visit to their newborn baby sister. When Bridget's water broke, we thankfully had some of our Australian extended family, the Richards, nested in the guest bedrooms, so we could take flight knowing the boys would be well tended.

Neither Bridget nor I had any inkling about the new baby's gender: not the foggiest if we'd get ourselves a boy or a girl beforehand, but we did know our child was going to be, CF-Free. The boys said they'd be pleased either way, but suggested, it would be cool if they could get themselves a baby sister. I knew Bridget would feel blessed if she had a daughter of her very own.

It was pitch black when I left Truckee Hospital's parking lot for home. A powdered snow started falling again on the pass. The roadside sign said we were at 7320 feet above sea level, and snow chains could on occasion be required. I was ahead of the plow and pulled off in the dark onto the chain-installation side lane, white dust-like snow blanketing everything around me.

The visual-pollution-free sky was clear and the local stars threatened to reach down and touch me on my Rubicon cap.

I left the Truckee Hospital in the dark, and a light powder of snowfall just blanketed everything. My tire tracks are the first ones on the road, and the night sky is overcrowded at this altitude with stars. On the pass I stop the Jeep and turn off the lights. No sound, nothing moving, just me hearing the sound of my own breath.

Our daughter Hayley is the most beautiful thing
I've ever laid eyes on, tucked up alongside Bridget. It
was one of the few times in my life I felt there must be
some kind of God because I could not have been more
blessed. First light began to show the outline of Lake
Tahoe, and I would go home to collect our two sons and
return to Bridget and our new baby. I am blessed beyond
any tool every created to measure my good fortune.

Today, I'll wait to give Cody son his postural
drainage, his 'thumping', until after we see his new sister.

– Journal entry, 10 January 1997

Cute kids!

One day when he was around ten years old, Dylan came home from school saying he wanted to do acting work, and Bridget started asking questions. It appeared that Dyl's new-found passion for pursuing a career in acting was inspired by one of his buddies from school who got entire days, sometimes even weeks off, because he was 'on location' for a film or ad 'shoot'. And, according to Dylan, the kid got paid big money for it too. Bridget did some asking around, and the next thing we knew, he was not only on the 'books' with an agent but was getting his wish of having his mom tote him all over town to auditions and 'work'. His pay was large for a kid, depending on the parts he played, and we agreed that any money earned was all his, but he was only to keep $50 mad money from each job. This would, years later, become a sticking point.

Meanwhile, Dylan landed a leading role in a major McDonald's campaign, which was monumental; it paid residuals to the 'leads' every time it was shown in the region. Central wardrobe asked us to bring him into the advertising agency on a Saturday, and we said we'd be along as soon as he finished his softball game. We arrived with the entire family in tow, as we were going away for the long weekend. When we arrived the place was organized chaos, 50 people all-up, kids and parents shifting from leg to leg, holding pees. The costuming director said 'Oh my God Dylan! Where have you been?! We've been waiting on you for the past hour!' Dylan was whisked away before I could slap the gal, and I calmly took a seat alongside Hayley.

Bridget, accustomed to the audition chaos, dutifully filled out another set of forms about how we'd need to care for the rags Dylan was about to be given for the shoot.

Lights, camera, kid sister!

Meanwhile, the rest of us hovered while Dylan was 'in wardrobe'. Sitting next to Hayley was an American gal with a clipboard, who started engaging Hayley in chatter, and they hit it off instantly. Hayley said she was not an actress, but her brother Dylan was, and the gal asked if she was Dylan Sheehan's sister. 'Yep! You bet!', Hayley fronted up with a smile and great pride of ownership in her brother. The American offered to show Hayley the camera set-up and turned to Bridget asking if she could borrow our daughter for a few moments; it wouldn't be long and if Hayley would feel better, one of us could go too.

Bridget asked Hayley, who said she could do it fine on her own and trotted off with her new friend through the crowd and into the studio. Fifteen minutes later they returned, and 'June' asked if Hayley had an agent. They wanted to sign her for the other 'lead' playing the part of Dylan's sister.

The original kid targeted for the role was a 'real brat' with a dominating mother to boot. And although 'June', who turned out to be the *director* out from the USA could not fire her, or alter her pay scale, she could, move her to an 'extra' role and swap Hayley into the co-lead role. *If* Hayley was keen to give it a go? Hayley again said 'Yep!', beaming! Back through the doors for a costume swap from the old kid to the new kid, and Hayley was on her way ...

Never, ever put life on hold!

Between Dylan and Hayley, they locked away some serious funds, but I think they had heaps of fun doing it. Bridget, who had given up plans for theatrics with other demands, loved getting involved. We still have the entire season of the Seven Network's *Backyard Science* program, with Hayley as co-host. When she was offered a spot on *Are You Smarter Than a 5th Grader?* without even doing a screen test she turned it down as it required her going to Melbourne for a few days of filming each month. Her agent tried repeatedly to change her and Bridget's thinking, to no avail. Work dried up after that. I know now, you don't say no to Hollywood, Hollywood says no to you.

Contract disputes! Dylan walks!

Dylan's departure from acting was a self-inflicted wound: he revolted at his remuneration. Despite his parents showing him the rapidly growing bank balance held for later years, he was keen on more in-hand gratification and we refused to give over the large sums of money from each job until he was older. He had other things on his agenda, and they seemed to be connected to girls, or skateboards, or his new passion for making music. He was writing his own lyrics and the acting, I think, was a distraction. I've forgotten the girl's name now ... His agent Gordon was very sorry to see Dylan go.

Enter Spielberg Sheehan! Captain Cody behind the camera

Cody was far more intent on being on the other side of the camera; he was infatuated with the notion of making films. He made three and collaborated on others and went off to NIDA (the National Institute of Dramatic Art) in Sydney for their director's program with some fancy-pants cameras and state-of-the-art editing gear he was awarded by the Starlight Foundation in the 8th grade when they heard his idol was Steven Spielberg.

I lucky!

At least once a year I watch the film *Forrest Gump* because I think sometimes sheer entertainment films do echo real life. Forrest was a determined dumb-ass who with inspiration from loved ones just pressed ahead and got some historical, even though fictional, shit done. In many ways, I'm a take-off on this film's notion: 'Run Forrest run!' A dumb-assed kid who kicked off his braces and learned to sprint. Momma says, 'Life *is*, like a box of chocolates. You never know what you're gonna get!'

'Dad! I'm having a backyard party'

For Hayley's seventeenth birthday party I was given a contract that required signatures, and witnesses as well:

> *This is Hayley's night, she is 17 and can handle it with a little help from her friends.*
>
> *I, Mark Sheehan, can stay inside, not wearing flip-flops. I will NOT drink beer or talk Hayley's friends' ears off.*
>
> *I will only go outside if invited by Hayley due to some reason.*
>
> *Hayley will tell me I am handsome and modest, and smart, and good-looking and will thank me infinitely.*
>
> *The dog must stay inside!*

There are three signatures on the contract – mine Hayley's and Cody's as witness – and one mock paw print for Texas-dawg.

CHAPTER 8

A True Friend to the End Leaps Quietly In

To this day, the covert campaign that my wonderful friend Chris Newman undertook on my family's behalf has remained unwritten.

Not even Chris's widow Jane had any inkling to how hard Chris worked to keep me and my family from having to return to the USA.

Chris, the managing director of Insight Tours insisted that our best tactic was for him to remain on the coalface, fully unconnected and unaffected by Bridget, or Cody, or my emotionally charged campaign to help keep *all* of us Sheehans in an Australian nest permanently. Chris figured he would fly, seemingly unaffected, under Insight's corporate radar and have more traction that way. He was, remarkably, right.

I did a lousy job for Chris's eulogy, delivered at St Mary's over 10 years ago now, and I'm sure he'd be okay with my loving disclosures now; we're beyond any emotional statute of limitations.

'Hire somebody else Chris! This guy's got way too much baggage!'

Insight Tours' accountant (I never liked the guy ...) had advised Chris that I was trouble, and he should stay well away from me. Screw that! In our very first meeting 'The Newman' and I clicked like the snap of your fingers. Chris was one of a kind, and his Insight Tours team loved and adored him. Chris had a dry, quick and quirky sense of humor, which should have landed him in litigation strife if his team didn't just love his antics.

Within the first hour of our negotiations, Chris agreed that Insight Tours would happily take on our TrekAmerica business in the Pacific as the general sales agents (GSA), arrange for my appointment as caretaker for the brand, and I'd have an office of my very own just down the hallway from him: 'Yanks are very loud on the phone' and he wanted to be able to close the door if I got overly enthusiastic. In truth, I learned later Chris was keen to relocate his nitpicking, bean-counting accountant into the stationery closet behind reception. I got *his* office. I was a welcomed catalyst for in-office changes. Sharks and whales have pilot fish that swim safely attached to them, cleaning up as they swim. I was happy to be Chris's pilot fish. If he wanted to spruce things up a bit, I was his go-to guy. That very same accountant, who got moved to the broom closet became a perfect example. During a managers and directors meeting, this bean counter openly outed me on the way in which I completed my expense account forms. Instead of cowering, I said it was impossible to find the right slot to put my expenses in … there wasn't even a category for hookers and alcohol! Everyone laughed, and it took the edge off for everyone but the bean counter. Chris leaned back in his chair, shook his head and suggested we review the expense template before the next meeting.

When I candidly pointed out the fact that I might have a bit of unique family excess luggage to relocate he called in his personal assistant, the lovely Wendy, and assured me the paperwork would not be a problem. Wendy too adopted Chris's gusto. She beamed and said, 'No worries Mark I'll get right on it!'

To import my arse to Australia to represent TrekAmerica, Insight had to fill out reams of paperwork, pay significant fees for me and my family, and advertise my job description to assure there was not an Australian candidate who could fit the bill locally as a 'North American travel SPECIALIST'. HR conducted interviews and paid for nationwide searches but in the end, it would have been close-to-impossible to locate a bloke with a cleft in the center of his chin. The Sheehans were awarded a two-year, renewable temporary work visa. In that time, I was meant to train my replacement, a bit like 'planned obsolescence'. That's what they do in Detroit when making automobiles. Out with the old, then in with the new. The one sticking point was that because of Cody's cystic fibrosis, we'd be required to post a $25,000 bond against his needing medical care during that time. Insight bellied up and paid it for us. The accountant threatened to resign, and Chris whole-heartedly supported him in the notion.

'I'm sure it'll look good, once you take it out of the box!'

Chris ticked all the boxes regarding my interest in being paid in US dollars. That way meant we could stay on top of the cost of Cody's medications. Together we created a template for my contract which, with commissions and incentives, would eventually make me the highest paid fella in the Insight establishment. For a time at least: until other Insighters started probing why the Yank was getting all the perks, and they weren't. I didn't know it at the time, but Chris was creating an incentive-based platform he was going to apply to his own remuneration a year later.

The paperwork was done seamlessly, and even bureaucratic hiccups seemed to simply disappear. When I collected my shiny new fully covered company car (it was a Volvo station wagon, loaded to the gills with airbags), I installed Bridget as the designated driver and bought myself an older, ugly, pea-green station car for commuting to the office. I was surrounded in our parking lot by Beemers, Alfa Romeos and the odd Lexus. Chris drove a big Jaguar sedan.

This singular act created an unbelievable uproar as other executives argued openly with having to share the car park with a rust bucket. According to the paperwork, I had to be the sole operator of the new, attractive corporate wheels.

Chris put a stop to this with a single scud-missile memo – any executive who was unhappy to share the space with my ugly wheels, please feel free to turn in their keys or park on the street. Bridget enjoyed being behind the wheel, with Cody soundly strapped into a high-tech car seat for our entire Insight tenure.

Cody loved going anywhere in the car, except for taking his dad to the airport. I was playing Vivaldi's *Four Seasons* in the backyard one time when Cody said he hated that music, it was making him sick. He asked me to turn it off; and please Dad, never play it while he was nearby. I promised and asked why. My little boy's reply shocked me. During countless trips to 'drop Dad off at the airport', I'd play Vivaldi in the car to soften my departures. Steady my reserve as to why I was abandoning my loved ones again. I detested leaving my family, sometimes for weeks on end, and dreaded saying goodbyes. I'd play the Vivaldi to pull the emotional covers over my head, which my kids learned to associate with my leaving home. AGAIN. For years after I left them at the curbside, I'd go straight to the toilet and vomit. Bridget worked hard to make up for my absences, and to soften the impact for me while I was away. I'd often find beautiful notes from her in my suitcase, and a kid's art and bit of schoolwork tucked in socks and underwear. She was the glue that kept me together. When I phoned home, my wife would make a big shout-out to the kids as if we'd just won the lottery: 'Kids, come quick Dad's on the phone!'

My phone bills from hotels everywhere were always significant; yet another sticking point for our Insight accountant. 'The Newman' said the only reason the bean counter even had a job and a company car was because of 'guys like us'. 'Sheehan's sales pay your salaries!'

They love us … they love us not!

Insight's lawyers were fast-tracked to gain us temporary residency, posted the $25,000 bond for our participation in Medicare, the public health scheme, and paid fully for transplanting the family from Charleston to Sydney. Again, Chris quietly doing his best behind-the-scenes work on behalf of the Sheehans.

I still have the official letter in a brown cardboard box somewhere from when we were accepted as permanent residents of Australia years later. The notice from Australian Immigration determined the country would be pleased to accept the entire Sheehan family as permanent residents, *with the exception of Cody!* Australia was happy to have us, if we could somehow leave our first-born son Cody out of the equation. 'The Newman' again supported what was to become a five-year campaign to get the entire Sheehan clan accepted. Bridget undertook the gargantuan task of dealing almost daily with the powers-that-be, assembling doctors' reports, X-rays, evaluations by medical examiners and more.

CHAPTER 9

Absolutely, Positively No Pets Please!

Almost all the people in the know, or materials we read, endorsed the notion that you should *not* have pets with a cystic fibrosis kid around. They say the same thing for folks with asthma. Having pets is out of the picture for a CF kid because of the hairs in the air, and everyone already knows cats and dogs like to lick their butts. Long before Bridget was pregnant with Cody, we lived in 'The Manor' on Staten Island, complete with tennis court, swimming pool and a constantly changing houseful of Trek leaders on 'turn-arounds' in between tours. It was a bit of a revolving Woodstock atmosphere, where Trek leaders could unwind, make nocturnal visits to the local bars with peers, complete paperwork and trek expenses and gear up for the next tour. The only two firm house rules were: never-ever bring a Trek passenger to the Manor, and no way, no how, were pets allowed.

One morning a mottled kitten appeared at our back door, apparently dumped in the surrounding woods, hungry and hunting for a handout. Bridget discreetly offered the little ball of starving fur a bowl of milk. Love at first sight. I firmly repeated the house mantra of absolutely NO PETS! And I was certain the message sunk in, as the kitten disappeared from the doorstep. Unbeknown to me and the revolving door of transient Trekkers, Bridget had other plans. Knowing the lay of the land in 'the Manor', she covertly contrived a secret cat passage into the basement, so the kitten could nest nightly on a comfy pillow behind the copy machine. She stowed smuggled food, fresh milk and water there as well. This Anne Frank arrangement went unnoticed for many weeks, until the cat elected to come out of the closet one morning and was found sleeping splayed happily across the kitchen table. All hell broke loose. The cat 'had to go' alarm bells rang loudly, a household emergency meeting was held, and Bridget put her lovely Namibian foot down: 'If the cat goes, I go!'

The rest is history; we rewrote the house rules to include 'Gurdy-cat' as the house mascot with full privileges to roam and curl up wherever she damn well pleased, and that cat slept at the foot of our bed nightly for many years afterwards. When we moved the office to the west coast Gurdy-cat flew with Bridget while I toted a truckload of our gear around the countryside … and back.

Waiting, curled up like a welcome mat in Cody's crib on the day we took him home from the hospital in Charleston was Gurdy-cat. The cat was 'grandfathered' in, and was going to stay, even after we were advised keeping pets around CF kids was not a good idea. That cat adopted our Cody as her own, like Bridget had adopted her.

Enter Texas dawg, stage left!

At some point when I was topping up on cystic fibrosis information, I read in a scientific paper that pets should be removed from households with CF patients. I thought, no worries, Gurdy was pushing up daisies in our Charleston garden by then, and we were, mostly, pet free. Okay, we'd been gifted two guinea pigs, named Harley and Davidson, but they spent most of their lives taking turns at going in circles on the metal treadmill in their outdoor cage. Being a gift from my kid sister Cathy, they were easy to send back when we went overseas on holiday. And they just stayed on the treadmill there at my sister's house, but we could visit any time we liked. My wonderful sister has been taking in strays her entire life. Like our mother, Cathy collected the seemingly homeless.

At that time, our happy household also hosted a small box turtle that lived in a specially designed plastic tray with an island/palm tree set up in the middle. The turtle would crap on your hand each time you palmed it. Knowing this, our kids would get newcomers and pajama-party stayovers to 'Go ahead, pick him up, he's friendly' (chuckle, chuckle! Kid conspiracy!).

The medical journal was referring mostly to recommendations to get rid of dogs or cats if you already had them and referring readers to other articles on dealing with the significant potential for emotional trauma surrounding pet separation. Acquiring pets would be completely, fully, without a doubt, out of the question.

'Put your mother on the phone!'

I took a call from my Princess Hayley, and the conversation went something like this:

'Dad, Dad! Guess what? We've got a puppy. Mom says it's okay, cause its only for overnight so the puppies don't have to stay alone in the dark pet shop. Dad! He's so cute, but don't worry, I'm not allowed to name him unless we buy him ...'

'Hayley, please, put your mom on the phone!'

'Sorry Dad, she's driving and said she'll tell ya all about it later ... Gotta go now Dad, this puppy is licking Dylan all over, it's so funny dad ...'

Bridget did call back to clarify things, which went a short distance to easing my anxiety. 'Mark, it's okay, I've told the kids that the puppy can only come home overnight, and it does not belong to us. We'll drop it back at the shop before they open at eight, on my way to drop the kids at school.'

'Thanks Bridget, but you know we agreed no more pets, with our travel plans, and Cody's CF and ...'

'Mark, I've got it, I just wanted to let the kids play with the puppy for the afternoon. It'll be gone by morning, promise.'

And Bridget kept hers. The puppy went right back in the pet shop window, there before eight in the morning.

At three the next day, Hayley called again, 'Guess what Dad?! The puppy didn't get sold during the day, so the shop said we could take him home again for the night 'cause we brought him back right on time today!'

'Hayley?! Please put your mom on the phone!'

'Sorry Dad, she's driving, she says she'll call you back later. Dad? The puppy loves Cody too, he's licking him all over, you won't believe it! Gotta go, love you Dad!' The phone went silent in my palm. I just looked at it for a while.

Bridget called back, which did a little less to relieve my anxiety than the previous day. 'Mark, it's all okay. The kids know the pet must be back tomorrow before eight. They were all there at the counter when the shopkeeper spelled out the overnight rules for visits. She also told the kids no puppies were ever allowed to stay more than three nights with the same family because it wasn't fair to the puppy, which'd be thinking this was its new home. So please, can you relax, I know we agreed to no pets now. I've got this under control.'

That evening, the puppy was curled up in Dylan's lap in front of the TV, his siblings were by his side, happily pointing to the puppy. Hayley put her finger to her lips, silencing me; she didn't want me to wake her puppy.

On the third day, in anticipation, I asked Joanna to put through any calls at all to our board room during the weekly marketing meeting. It was almost to the minute I got Hayley's call: 'Daddy, don't even ask to talk to mom right now, she's driving. But she told me to tell you, we know, we know, the puppy has to go back tomorrow and we can't have it visit after that again. Dad, it jumped all over the cage in the store when it saw Cody just now. He so excited he peed. No! Not Cody, the puppy. But Cody did flap his hands around like he does when he gets excited.' I didn't even bother to ask my daughter to put her mother on the phone.

That evening, I was down on Peppercorn Drive talking to my neighbor, when Hayley came running up, tears streaming down her face, screaming. The puppy was dead and stopped breathing and its neck was busted. I sprinted up the drive to find Bridget giving mouth-to-mouth to the puppy and using two fingers as a way to compress its chest. With the puppy wrapped in a blanket on Bridge's lap, we flew out of the driveway, headed for the vet. The last thing I saw in the rear-view mirror was our three crying children, fear in their eyes. I ran red lights and made record time to the hospital where the vet was waiting in the lot. By the time we got to the front door, the unnamed puppy had begun to revive, and was merrily licking Bridget's hand. While I was interrogated by the vet, Bridget called home to tell the kids all the signs were good.

Thing is, the puppy seemed to have made a full and frisky recovery as the vet felt him over. He was soaking the vet with licks, tail wagging while being examined. The tone and questions I was being asked by the vet began to vex me. How was it that I did not even know what kind of dog we had? Or what the dog's name was? Or how old it was? The clear implication seemed to be that I, in conspiracy with my loved ones, had somehow abused the puppy. It felt as if the vet was getting ready to safeguard and seize the dog, while making a full-on citizen's arrest. I was being emotionally prodded and was clearly under suspicion. Perhaps under the same interrogation light as child molesters or east African elephant poachers. The final stinger came when the vet reluctantly returned the puppy to Bridget's blanket and advised me that the emergency visit would cost $147 instead of the regular $40 tariff. We'd arrived at the door at 7.04 pm and were to be billed the after-hours rates. Had we been a singular minute before seven, I'd have paid $107 less for the exact same services.

On the way home, I regaled Bridget with all the reasons we did not have space in our lives for a puppy, in any condition. The kids cried when we got home, only this time they were tears of pure joy. I sunk into our bed, totally emotionally exhausted.

Over family breakfast, I confirmed with Bridget and the kids that the puppy would be returning to the pet shop, and although they were disappointed a deal was a deal. Bridget told me to relax, she'd drop the kids off at schools, and as promised she'd take the pooch back to the retailer. Bridget kept her promise.

Another call, that, changed it all!

> At 3.09 today I took a call from Hayley, and before I could lever a word in edgewise, she said: 'Dad, Dad! Guess what!? We bought the puppy! And don't worry about where its gonna sleep cause Mom just bought a big doghouse, and sleep mat and ...' I held the phone away from my ear, regained my footing and said as calmly as I could while panting for air, 'Put your mother on the phone!'

Bridget had kept her promise, reluctantly returning the nameless pooch to its pen in the pet shop. Her heart was broken because she felt the bond had been established with this puppy. All through the day it kept haunting her, and she collected Hayley from school early and raced to the shop. It was in the hands of the 'fates', and if it was still unsold the puppy belonged in our home. The tiny, multicolored pooch had spoken to her. We needed this dog in our lives.

The kids promised to train, and clean, and look after the dog as long as they lived and named him Texas. With a heart and spirit as big as Texas, that puppy embedded itself in all our hearts for years upon years upon years. I wept openly when I had to carry him in my arms for the very last time to his resting place in our backyard. And I wept silently for weeks after his passing. He was, for all of us, good medicine for the heart that no doctor could have ever prescribed.

Heavy petting!

Cody has always had a take-'em-or-leave-'em attitude towards our pets, which I find remarkable, as they are totally loyal, and seek him out constantly. The cat would seize any opportunity to curl up at his feet, or anchor herself at the foot of his bed. Texas dog sat vigil at the front door window, scanning the lawn while waiting for his safe return. The dog would invade his room, leap onto his bed and be completely content to just sleep there through an entire day if allowed, and if he was flicked, he'd just as happily tuck in under the bed, awaiting further instruction.

I often kid our kids about this unwavering loyalty on the part of our pets, as I have always been the go-to guy when it comes to walks, feeding, bathing cleaning-up after the spilling of the garbage pails across the kitchen floor and more. Picking up poops in degradable plastic bags. And yet, our pets adhered themselves like super glue to the kids. On evenings when they couldn't invade Cody's domain, both Texas and 'Scratch-cat' would make do in my bed linen and complain bitterly if I made the smallest of adjustments to get comfortable; when Cody gave the kitty a nudge, she purred like the kitten she once was. For her, a nudge from our son was more like a caress, even though Cody would often suggest he could care less. Secretly, I think he was lying.

Having pets in our lives has been proven to enhance our quality of life and longevity

We once put one of those idiot-looking dunce cones around Texas-dog's neck to keep him from licking his paws, and Princess Hayley had him convinced he looked handsome. He'd strut around the neighborhood like a king in new clothes, and might have consented to wear the plastic mane forevermore, if he'd only had a way to lick his butt.

The experts might have said that pets were not advised in a cystic fibrosis household, but nobody was saying anything about how pets can create a glue of their very own magic in the making.

Following in Gurdy's paw-prints came many other pets. Oreo, Ruby and Scratch were cats who enjoyed having our family as staff. Scratch still runs roost here and would even let Texas dog think he was the boss from time to time. And let us not forget Harley and Davidson the guinea pigs, or the rapidly reproducing 'food fish' that Hayley and I rescued for 50 cents apiece.

Texas-dog had a habit of raiding Cody's bag, which he discovered had an entire arsenal of good chocolates and individually wrapped crackers. He never seemed to tear into them, but preferred to bury them for another time, only to forget where they'd been hidden. Cutting the lawn, I'd find a stash of potato chips along the back fence, or running the vacuum, I'd find something jamming the suctioning power significantly, only to discover a small, beyond its use-by date Snickers bar in the throat of the machine.

The Texas terrorist on four legs took to hiding his treasures under Cody's pillow, or in the pile of laundry that seemed to accumulate at the foot of Cody's bed. Maybe the dog, like me, was just dropping reminders for Cody to beef up, whenever the opportunity arose. Most cystic fibrosis kids struggle to keep on weight, and I was constantly covertly trying to find new snacks to attract Cody's attention. Cody rarely snapped at his old man, when I nagged the shit out of him about taking enzymes, or not eating enough. Maybe his dog was just trying to help, and I must admit, the puppy took great pain not to perforate the wrappers. One night Cody's mask went missing, a real mystery to everyone but the dog. The mask turned up under the sofa days later, alongside a warren of other items the dog had hidden: his wooden handled brush and an American Mars candy bar sent to Cody though the mail by one of the 'cystas' in the USA. I'm still not sure where Texas found the packet of Pop Tarts.

Swiping the mask was the best way Texas had of saying

enough is enough, and even Cody's dog seemed to be saying, he was ready for a cure. Some birds will steal shiny items or bits of thread to admire at a later date or use in the making of an attractive nest. Texas stole stuff that he hoped would never be found again.

Perceptive pets!

Texas may officially have been Dylan's dog, and the cats officially the property of other siblings, but when it came to the kids the pets were the bosses. Days before I got a notion that some bad stuff was happening on the homefront, Texas dog had already set up a sentinel's spot at our son's bedroom door. He'd stay there, foregoing treats or the call to the tin bowl for his dog food, or even water, until Cody opened his door. Texas stretched his small, terrorist-on-four-legs frame across the path so none might enter or, more importantly, exit without his notice.

When Cody alighted, Texas would blanket the undercarriage of Cody's kitchen chair while our son checked Facebook for obituaries and bad news, mixed with miracles and messages from his worldwide peers. Cody calls them his 'cystas' and 'fibros' and his CF Avengers buddies. If Cody so much as stretched, his Texas dog was underfoot to check on his pathway. Through the bedroom door, he could hear Cody struggle to breathe, and if he could speak, I'm sure that dog would say something like, 'You're his father, pick him up in your arms, and deliver him to the place where the doctors and nurses can fix him again.' If life were only this simple.

When Texas knew any of his children were sick, it significantly upset him.

Kids *do* need pets ... and pets need our kids.

> *Texas-dog knows when Cody's not doing well. This morning he camped under my son's bed, refusing to be lured away even with treats on offer. He's like the canary in the coal mine and knows when the air is bad. This morning it was very, very bad. Like me, Texas had heard our Cody coughing through the walls last night at length and slept sentinel-like at his bedroom door. We both knew Cody was not going to pull up from this current nosedive without help from the tower. Cody knew it too, but he was stalling. He's come to disdain the needed hospitalizations which get in the way of his attempt to just live a normal life.*

CHAPTER 10

School Daze |

When Cody was an infant, Bridget and I declined all overtures to have our son treated as if he were handicapped. We were determined that Cody should, as much as possible, run, jump, and spit like the other kids and participate fully in just being a kid. We made the choice to refuse social security benefits, handicapped parking privileges, and other insulating options. Instead, we elected to mainstream our son and find schools and opportunities that would allow Cody to engage in the playground and in class, while allowing for his multiple hospital admissions.

Bridget finding and insisting on Montessori and Steiner schools not only smoothly integrated him into his world but led us as a family to the best parents, other wonderful children and teachers who could be candidates for cloning, and our rock-fast future friends. Cody would puff up like a peacock, boasting that he had 'two other mothers', both of whom adopted him and his siblings through those open-hearted schools.

'Everything happens for a reason' – Bridget

Back in Charleston, I got a call from one of the partners in a law firm I looked after: my startup Publicity Plus had launched a flight plan that put this trio of founding lawyers on the path to five other satellite offices across two states. I was, in the eyes of these blokes, a golden boy when I took the call. The short bit of the conversation was that this bankruptcy lawyer's wife was threatening to divorce him *if* her children's Montessori school was forced to close for lack of admissions. He put me on the board, and his firm agreed to pay my fees in the event the school went belly-up. We created some fabulous programs, in which Bridget got intimately involved, including our cleverly created recruitment of kids with Sundaes on Sundays! Prospective families were invited to come for a play on Sundays, and the kids could create ice-cream delights with the help of current students and their parents. Kids made new pals and parents talked among themselves, and enrollments went through the roof. We did other events to let prospective parents see just how wonderful educating a kid might be at Montessori.

1991ish living in paradise – the 'lucky country'

When I first uprooted our family of three to Australia, we had only my sister and kid-brother Chris living in the lucky country. And Chris was happily anchored in Brisbane, while my sister Cathy was a solid hour or more away from our new nest, because of my office location and the proximity to potential Montessori schools for our son.

Bridget was packing up our home in Charleston, selling up cars and finding tenants for our place there. I'd wanted to sell, and Bridget insisted that we keep the house on Henrietta Street. My only real assignment as the advance guard, was to find a home within driving distance of a Montessori campus, close to shopping and with an electric garage door opener so Bridget could return from outings with the stroller, two boys and groceries without having to exit the family station wagon.

And I found the perfect place, dead center between the two potential schools on Griffith Street in Fairlight in Sydney. I made the deal on the spot, sending Bridget Polaroids of the level back yard, lovely leaded glass windows, vaulted Victorian ceilings and a significant two-car garage with electric door opener. Yep, I nailed it: 'The largest shopping center in the Southern Hemisphere is nearby!' according to the real estate agent. She lied, and what I neglected to reveal to Bridget when I sent the pictures was the teeny-tiny fact that the new family headquarters had a few significant steps to climb *between* the garage and the stained-glass front door: 87 of them to be precise! Locally, the spot was known as the 'Eagle's Nest'. Nobody's perfect.

Always check the details but, fortunately for me, there was a shopping center nearby which did carry all the right stuff and enough shops and kids' play areas to get me a passing evaluation of this front. Later, this would be critical to the survival of my marriage when Bridget informed me that the Woolworths grocery store delivered to the front door for only $5 a clip for up to six bags.

I think if Bridget could have buried my body without detection while caring for our two kids, she would have done me in after seeing the place for the first time. Apart from the 87 uneven stone steps to the front door, the bountiful balcony loomed over a somewhat unsafe 50-foot drop and we later learned that the well-fenced backyard was prone to infestation by funnel-web spiders and snakes. The fence apparently served to keep them all in. And, of course, there were the three ample bedrooms with plenty of unencumbered light, which made the place a pizza oven in summer, and allowed for a wind-tunnel effect of cold blasts during the winter. Our first summer in that house, the nearby bushfires blocked out the sun for days on end, and you could almost cut the smoke with a butter knife. That year nearly 2500 bush firefighters battled more than 30 blazes around the state and 14 homes were destroyed.

Bushfires – I get what it feels like to breathe through a straw

Tonight I'm up, on the front porch of the Griffith Street place and the sky is loaded with fluttering, insect-like embers. They flicker under the streetlights, butterfly-like. The forest fires have been raging for days now, and the sunrises are stark maroon reds and oranges. I can feel the smoke at the back of my throat, and although we keep the kids indoors, the forest burning is everywhere, permeating even our clothes, as if we'd spent a weekend camping and roasting marshmallows in the Catskills. I wonder how my son's lungs will deal

with another day of these constant fireplace inhalations.
Even on good days, he seems to struggle to the top of
the monkey bars.

– Journal entry, October 1991

Adapting to whatever leaf you are sitting on – become a chameleon!

Bridget, thankfully, is very adaptive and, I must say, fabulously forgiving. After all, the new place was close to Manly Beach, one of Australia's best. Mind you, it was about a one-mile hike straight up a broken-concreted sidewalk, laboring a tandem stroller to get home after a day of play on the sand, which was not an option. Thankfully the council offered two hours free underground parking.

The redeeming feature about the place was its location; it was within easy distance to not one, but two, potential Montessori schools. This was not only a priority on my shopping list of finding us a home, but it sat at the very top! We could merrily do without walk-in closets, or a pool, or views of the Pacific or the Opera House *but*, getting Cody into a Montessori classroom was critical to my marriage.

I visited both schools, schmoozed the headmasters, and subtly suggested under-the-table donations as a lure to Cody's enrollment, only to be told there was at least a six-month waiting list, and Cody would be at the bottom of a list numbering in the double digits for admission.

My heart sank when I told Bridget, the odds didn't look good for Cody starting at a Montessori any time soon. Bridget had been ready to tackle my next adventure alongside me, but there was a limit to her enthusiasm with two young boys to raise while I flitted about the planet chasing sales for the new business venture.

Miracles do happen, some of them, mother-made!

We were given a fully furnished apartment overlooking the Sydney Harbour Bridge for as long as it took for our sea-going container of belongings to arrive, but both Bridget and I wanted to be in the new place, and we bought a sofa bed (not recommend for a bad back!), a few stout folding chairs and a kitchen table and moved into the 'Eagle's Nest', making it our own.

And then Bridget began working her magic; she visited the nearest Montessori with our sons, spoke to the wonderful Wendy who was the Irish-born headmistress, and spilled the beans on how much it would mean to us to have our kids under her wing. Two days later Bridget got a call saying they'd found a loophole in the admissions policy for overseas transplants, and a place had miraculously opened up. Bridget was class mother thereafter, helped in the classroom weekly, and we soon discovered an entire army of extended family, which we share to this day. Our closest friends were created through our children, new business partners revealed themselves, and countless holidays, memories and backyard barbecues have been graced by this single gesture of acceptance. I'm a walking sandwich board for the parents and teachers who feel that educating their children should be an adventure and a journey they will cherish for an entire lifetime.

Before I laid eyes on Cody, I was determined to have our child educated in a top private school, one that returned a solid baseline in reading, writing and arithmetic. If boarding schools and strict discipline were the path to future success, I was going to throw money at the schoolmarms. Imagine my surprise when Cody's teacher told me to 'slow down' and stop trying to teach Cody the ABCs. Learning to read was an adventure, where the letter 'A' was weaved as a tapestry of stories surrounding King Arthur and the knights of the round table. And I must confess, they were so very right!

My extended family – Cody

> *Our school mothers were exceptional at getting our families together outside the classroom. I think they liked each other's company and saw camping trips for the troops, extended convoy weeks at Diggers Beach and other outside-of-school-hours activities as a way of melding us all together. We've been beautifully fused as one, remarkable extended family, joined together at the emotional ankles.*

Batman and Robin come to blows – by mistake!

Our backyard featured a Hill's Hoist, a sturdy-built clothesline that enabled the person hanging laundry to stay in one place while the 'lazy Susan' line spun around in a circle and it was perfect for tethering a rope swing for the boys to play on. One Easter Sunday, Bridget advanced on the backyard, modestly concealing chocolate eggs while our sons dressed in their holiday outfits with help from me – Cody elected to dress as Batman, sporting rubber gumboots and Dylan, always following his older brother's lead, got fully decked-out in his Robin outfit, both complete with the appropriate capes. As they collected chocolate Easter eggs for their baskets, Bridget filmed Cody's circumnavigation of the clothesline right up until the point of contact with Dylan's head. She also captures me poaching the same eggs, and dropping them like breadcrumbs in our wake, so it appeared the Easter bunny had left a zillion eggs. We would watch the rolling footage of this event annually and laugh our asses off with each viewing.

This house speaks to me. I really think we could make a home here

On the ride to the airport – Vivaldi's *Four Seasons* playing softly in the background – Bridget said, 'I'd like to start looking for a house Mark.'

I replied, while accelerating, 'Sure, start looking, but can't this conversation wait until I'm back? Let's talk it over when I'm home again, but in theory, if you want a new place, I'm all-in for discussing the notion.'

I was hosting about 25 of our top-selling agents to a nine-day trip to Turkey, with all the bells and kebabs and whirling dervishes laid on heavily (handcrafted Persian carpets were tossed in too!). Insight called it 'Our Top Ten!' to celebrate the agents who rang our cash registers the loudest. Legal baksheesh.

When I walked into our hotel in Istanbul, the well-dressed general manager raced forward, insisting that I 'Must phone home urgently, at any hour! Please Mr Sheehan, your wife just called!'

My pulse raced, and I imagined the worst. I abandoned my VIP guests and darted to my room with a view of the Blue Mosque, while I imagined a horrific scene on the homefront. Here I was playing, while back home … I was certain something dreadful had happened to either Cody or Dylan, or to Bridget … or maybe even all three. Placing the call took many minutes, which with my creative imagination, seemed like hours. I'd already envisioned burning infernos, tragic head-on car crashes and worse.

I was jotting down a rapid retreat plan on the hotel's bedside pad: how to grab the next flight, who'd take over the post position with my key customers, and whom I would call on back in Australia to fill in while I was en route. At best, I was 25 hours away from my loved ones.

Bridget answered the phone, sleep in her voice and I started in at full tilt.

'Please don't sugar-coat anything Bridget, I'm on the next flight. Who is it, Cody or Dylan? And you? Are you okay? When Bridget cut through and said, 'Mark, it's 1 am here, relax the kids and I are fine! I wanted to know where the checkbook was. I found a house today that spoke to me and the kids and I didn't want anyone else to get it.'

I do have an overactive imagination and have been described as a popsicle on the outside, but an extreme worry wart on the inside. I take blood pressure pills now, daily.

On my first inspection I hated the place: it was too small and would require significant upgrading, but I saw how the property felt like a future homestead for the Sheehans. For Cody and Dylan, it boasted a huge backyard, a view that revealed nothing but national park and, after all, it 'spoke to Bridget'. I was determined to get it, even if was over my budget and under my expectations.

While Bridget and the boys played on the tire swing in the backyard, I verbally tore into the realtor. I wanted *out* of this contract. Everywhere I looked the place needed something which needed lots of money or sweat to accomplish. Two new bathrooms, a new kitchen, a full-on fence in the backyard to separate kids from 1000 acres of national park ... the punch list in my head went on for pages. In the car afterwards, Bridget beamed, saying again that the house 'spoke to her'. I phoned the agent, and counteroffered on the price, which Bridget had already engineered at a $25,000 reduction. I said that I was flying again in 24 hours, so if he wanted to sell us a house, he'd better do it quickly. He made a call and advised us we'd just bought ourselves a house.

My first installation was a solid fence in the backyard, separating us from the 1000 acres of national park critters. My friends helped me erect it, and we drank a heap of beer in the process. Friends and family came around, admired the view and the kids played on the tire swing. The very next week I called a kid who'd put up a flier in the local supermarket, asking him to cut back scrub and trees that would let a bushfire leap the new fence easily. The kid wanted to be paid in cash, and I agreed, as long as he took any cuttings away with him when he went.

Cody and Dylan answered the front door, shortly after Dylan had tried to ride his trike down the three-turn stairway in our new place. 'Dad, Dad it's a park ranger, come quick!' Dylan sported a bruise across the bridge of his nose, but there was no blood.

At our front door was a National Parks officer. He held up an aerial photograph of the state's property and our block, pointing out the clear invasion of my tree felling and 'unauthorized' deforestation of public lands. A serious matter of vegetation violations.

It seemed the chap I hired from the IGA grocery store got carried away with his chainsaw and took a big bite out of the parkland in the process! I explained this misunderstanding to the ranger, while holding an icepack to Dylan's face, as Cody hovered around the officer, making note of his uniform. Cody liked to flap his hands as a kid when he got excited; like air-drying them, even if they weren't wet. I always loved his open display of excitement when he did this. He later asked if he and Dylan could have a park ranger uniform. I promised to 'look into it'. At the time Cody was wearing a Batman outfit and cape, Dylan was wearing a Robin Halloween costume.

I explained how the mistaken massacre of vegetation came to pass, and showed the flier to the ranger, who took the details and seemed satisfied to pursue his investigation with new evidence. I did call the kid who did the cutting to alert him of the ranger's visit and his reply was rather calm. 'No worries mate, I'm headed back to Queensland tomorrow now that I've got a bit of cash in me pocket. I'll just tell the fella politely like ta go fuck himself!'

A week later an entire bush-regeneration team rocked up, took away all the kid's abandoned cuttings, and pleasantly planted new, ankle-high stuff. They were all volunteers. Bridget and the kids toted them iced tea. We never did hear back from the ranger. Or the kid.

Eating out!

Oddly enough, the things that are good for CF kids to eat and digest to compensate for lousy absorption and a decaying digestive tract are *not* the best food groups for a dad to eat in large quantities. Cody's diet included extra fat content, and almost any eats that went into him without enzymes came out in a similar manner. Only a lot riper to the nose! When I was eating the food I cooked for Cody, I jumped a fair few waist sizes. Juggling the depth-charge-like explosive pancreatic enzymes our son was taking to win the battle of malnutrition in a small CF body was a bit like determining the number of grains in a section of sandpaper: take too many and the liver, spleen, kidneys and stomach take a beating; Take too few and all that goodness heads straight into the toilet – literally.

I got fat, while Cody treaded water with his weight. As Bridget has said for years by way of explanation, Cody was slim to start, having a generic disposition to this, as her parents had tried to fatten her up as a child. My story was similar, with our mother making special milkshakes during my kid-hood, to try and put some meat on my bones. I always attributed this to a very fast metabolism.

Today, Cody's pals, aunts and uncles, nice nieces and nephews have created an elaborate list of things they like to eat or cook and time them to coincide with Cody's invasions. His Aunt Cathy does her brilliantly wonderful double-baked potatoes with crispy cheese toppings – I just look cross-eyed at one and I've gained an entire kilo! I often eat two. They good! Auntie Ellie creates her famous spaghetti and meatballs in red sauce (the *only* red sauce Cody will 'ever' eat) and Auntie Anne makes a rich potato soup, which has no right to call itself soup because you simply can't sip the stuff – you need a small shovel to get through its weight-seeking special ingredients. Oddly enough, Cody can't stand soup of any kind. With this one exception. Alongside calorie-enriched eats, we purchased for years, trays of Ensure Plus, a fortified nutrition booster Cody drinks through a tiny straw attached to the side of each box. For every carton he drank, one pancreatic capsule slid along with it.

Junior entrepreneur! Cody's first franchise

I'm a stickler for having well shined shoes, a habit I developed shining the family shoes alongside my father. On Sundays, our dad would have each of the six Sheehan siblings deliver our Buster Brown's to the formica-topped kitchen table, where he'd laid down a layer of the Cleveland *Plain Dealer* or the *New York Times* as a protective condom and we'd, all of us Sheehans, sit side-by-side, applying the polish. Then buffing with the brush and adding the final gloss to our footwear with a kitty-soft chamois. There's an art in shining a shoe properly.

Cody, as a kid, took this to heart, especially when I added the incentive of two bucks for the boots: a buck a boot. The next thing I knew, his mother grabbed a complimentary brown box from the local wine merchant up the hill, and Cody had done some artwork to paste on its side. 'Shoe Masters!' Scrawled in kid art as advertising. He then went door to door on Derna Crescent, telling our neighbors he was open for business, and our kitchen table was soon populated with polish, school shoes and a smorgasbord of high heels and hiking boots. Cody charged a skinny two dollars a pair, and before long his reputation expanded to the next street corner and beyond. As his boot-buffing business grew, Cody hired his kid-brother Dylan as back-of-house support, and to help make sure the right shoes went back to the right feet and neighborhood front door.

Our boys were hauling in over 30 dollars a week when Cody's gal pal, cute Freya, said she might like to try the same thing in her neighborhood. Overnight Cody went from being a sole proprietor with an under-the-radar operation, to a franchise. He began decorating other cardboard wine tote boxes, providing the cleaning and polishing contents required to do the right thing by right and left feet, and was selling his concept to other kids in his class. The new tariff was $3 a pair. Two bucks for Freya, and a dollar for Cody-son. Cody got good at accomplishing his polishing, staying in touch with his franchisees, and simultaneously shining shoes while watching TV with his nebulizer mask on. Cody got 'thumped', doing postural drainage to clear his lungs twice every day during his entire childhood. That took about four hours every single day of the week. Shining shoes while doing the nebulizers, enabled the kid to learn a bit of multitasking! It took the edge off what to do with his hands.

The thin edge of the wedge!

I arrive home tonight and Dylan meets me at the front door. 'Dad, Cody got a new wedge today!' I think my son might be overreacting to the purchase of a new shoe wedge for his Shoe Masters campaign, until I see Cody bent over a massive yellow and orange foam ramp, a wedge designed to keep Cody's butt up, while keeping his head down during postural drainage. It encourages all the jelly-like gunk and junk that tries to smother him daily to flow with gravity. In this way, a CF kid can more successfully cough out the glue-like sputum which clogs the cilia of the lungs. All the glug goes into a mid-sized pile of tissue or a pint-sized toss-away cup. Cody currently coughs up and dumps more than 2 kilos, easily, each week like this.

Bridget was thumping Cody, who was very excited about having his new ramp working so well. I can tell because Cody flaps his hands like an accelerated queen's wave on a cartload of caffeine. Dylan would later try to jump his trike over the wedge unsuccessfully, before launching himself down the stairway to see if that might be fun. Dylan Thomas has the making of a future Evil Knievel, I think.

Cody gets thumped at least three times a week by visiting physios. The rest of the week either Bridget or I, or one of Cody's 'other mothers' chip in. If there were a new, better treatment, or gizmo out there for Cody's treatment, his mother would find it. I was inwardly thankful every time we got a new medication, or learned a better treatment technique at home, or Doc Morton suggested a new drug that might help with quality of life or longevity.

– Journal entry circa 1995

Outdoor adventures

We took the kids and their cousin Eloise camping, to field test the new 12-man tent I'd bought at a bargain. Sometimes a tent is just too well priced to let loose, even if you already own a few of them. The packing bag for the tent was torn, and it was already marked down by half when the manager said, 'Give us 200 bucks and it's yours!' He was tired of looking at it. I can never pass up a bargain, even if I don't need or want the thing on offer. We went north, with the promise of board games, spooky stories and even, fat, marshmallows to melt over an open fire.

What they didn't tell me, until we opened the 12 pages of owner's manual, was 'some assembly required' was nothing short of a bold-faced lie. An advanced degree in engineering was required. Thankfully, when we were setting up our new synthetic home away from hearth, we had Bridget and Eloise along and in command.

I was happy to fill the role of the enthusiastic lift-and-tote lad, alongside the boys. Hayley fed the birds from the sideline, handed her wonderful cuz tent stakes, and held tight to the directions from a perch on the nearby wooden-rail fence. The thing was spacious, and from our tent site I could run an extension cord, which meant we could play Monopoly while Cody did his nebulizer indoors. It was all a bit of 'Cadillac camping' and I remember taking a mental Polaroid of the setting to recall years later.

The skies opened up at night, and all the walls and floor of our tent began to weep. We tightened ourselves to the center pole to stay dry. I should have read the directions about spraying all the seams with a waterproofing sealer before use, and so it was only after the start of a three-day gale that I learned my lesson. Cody's nebulizer 'shorted out', all our sleeping bags were soaked, and we huddled, six of us in our palatial 12-man tent, on the only high ground inside like rodents on a sinking ship. I was reminded of a little plastic habitat I got for my turtle as a kid, with a raised island in its center, one lone and broken plastic palm tree for cover.

Extended family excursions – our children's 'other parents'

Not all our camping adventures ended in deluges. Together with our wonderful Montessori school friends, on many occasions our families would pack up and light out for camping gatherings, communal meals, kids climbing trees, mock-drowning each other and picnic table games in national parks. The parents were always keen to join in, or at least be on hand for the occasional application of bandaids. Our kids would play cards and board games for hours under a single camp lantern, often with Cody on his nebulizer, with an extension cord we'd connect to the cigarette lighter in someone's car. Not a single kid had a mobile phone, or even wanted one.

Sleepovers

Cody and Dylan, as kids, often had sleepovers in our home, with pals doubled up on bunk beds, and sprawled akimbo on the floor. They'd cook a barbecue dinner, play board games, and the backyard took a beating on the flying fox and rope swing. Our front yard was littered with a collection of bicycles and skateboards.

A regular stay-over was the lovely lass, Freya, who had Cody's life well-planned out before he got to the third grade. They were going to be married straight after completing elementary school, then pack up and go to Egypt, a place that held infinite fascination for them both. They'd spend hours looking over a coffee-table book of the maze-work of the pyramids, the clothing and jewelry of the Pharaohs, the papyrus boats that plied the Nile. It was either that, or Marvel comic-book heroes and heroines. Cody would flap his hand excitedly a lot when Freya was around.

These little recollections, with our son's friends, reaffirmed the notion that Cody was living a good-as-it-gets kid-hood. His pals never once balked at his having to take a break for nebulizers or get a postural drainage thumping. His future-wife Freya even learned to give Cody his thumpings, which for them morphed into a game of sorts as she pounded out and sang in beat to a *Sesame Street* song they both loved. Many of Cody's good buddies didn't grasp Cody's CF until they invaded their late teens. Neither did Cody. Cody got so good at discreetly downing four, five, or six enzyme capsules without detection, that I'd often have to ask him, using 'signs', if he'd taken them. Even years later, I'm still asking how he does it.

Five feet apart! Better make that six!

When Cody was young, we had been making plans for him and Bridget to attend a specially created CF summer camp for other cystic fibrosis families. A melting pot of CF kids and families from all over North America to make the most of what they got. Even families who might not have been able to afford a traditional 'vacation' were encouraged, and discreet donations and funding were provided to encourage the idea. We'd read all the literature about the fun stuff they did there, and how it helped CF kids bond and 'just breathe' among other kids born with CF. It was family-friendly so other siblings could mix in and Bridget was already investigating ways she could go along, chip in and be involved to help out during the week.

Almost overnight, with new study and research revelations, all that changed. Suddenly, like the turning of the key in the lock, medical practitioners and research teams from all points of the compass started screaming for CF families to stop packing, posthaste, and stop sharing close spaces. No more Camp CF. Putting CF kids within feet of each other was a hugely *bad, down-right-rotten idea*.

Mingling CF patients and their coughs had seemed harmless enough; after all, CF was a genetically transmitted disease. You can't really 'catch' it from somebody. But nobody really stopped to think much about the airborne, or saliva-toting toxins. A regular-type cough travels at 78–122 miles an hour (125–196 kilometres an hour), while a sneeze can zip along at over 200! So the reality of cross-infecting kids in the same place was in fact, a horrifically bad idea.

Even when Cody's doing well, he can cough a half dozen

times an hour during the day; multiply that by 12 hours and it covers a lot of ground. I did the calculations, while waiting for the boarding call to my Johannesburg flight. It's a lot.

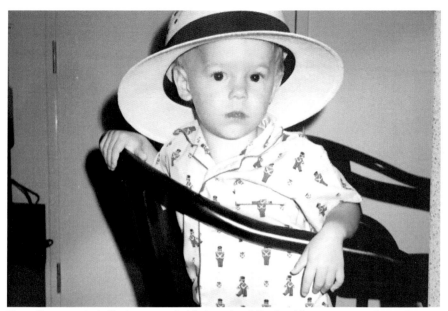

From the very start, Cody seemed able to extract the best from everyone he met. Sometimes that included nicking his Uncle Jim's hat.

Family first. Bridget and I were never really alone: we were surrounded by loved ones and people who cared.

Cody's best buddy Dylan rides the IV pole as Cody takes to the hospital hallways.

'Mark! Really? A BMW? We still have five more cities to get to, and then there's New Zealand!' — Bridget

Even before we helped launched V Australia, we conjured up all manner of ways to raise awareness and a whole lot of money to fight CF, including the Great Escape Oz car rally.

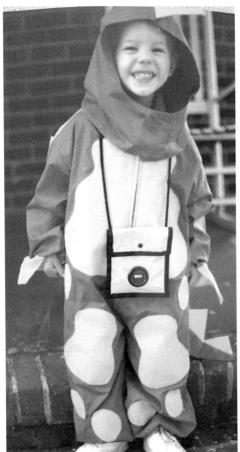

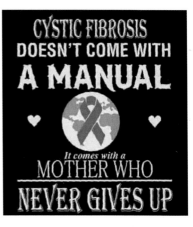

CYSTIC FIBROSIS
DOESN'T COME WITH
A MANUAL

It comes with a
MOTHER WHO
NEVER GIVES UP

Cystic fibrosis is not contagious; Cody's smile is! On the day Cody was diagnosed, the statistics were stacked against him living long enough to attend primary school. Somebody forgot to tell Cody's mom … and Cody.

Cody's siblings, Hayley and Dylan are his best pals.

The anti-smoking campaign won awards!

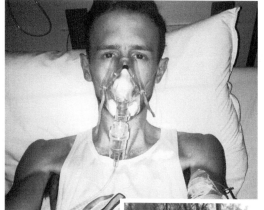

Dylan asked Doc Morton why his big brother had to wear that mask to breathe. The good doc said, 'Cody has CF, which means he has to breathe through a straw.' Later that day, Dylan peeled his 'Maccas' straw out of its wrapper and tried it. Some days I had to force myself to wait for my tears until after I left Cody's bedside.

The Capt's cronies. Jack Aakhus, aka 'Action Jackson', and Cody's bestie Cairyn Bloomfield, aka 'gym wife'.

I honestly don't know how Cody keeps up with the thousands of his fellow 'cystas' and 'fibros'.

Cody always had lots of support from his friends. Pictured here with his kid sister Hayley.

Social media and Facebook connect Cody to an entire planet of CF friends and their families. Some days I adored the connections, other days I dreaded the horrific news of another CF pal who could no longer wait.

Australia's Prime Minister heralded Cody's transplant team's success. Malcolm Turnbull called it, 'a medical miracle, the marriage between public and private hospitals.' Cody's mom, ever-present in the background.

"I don't let CF define me"

I detest this photo. Cody insisted on going to the CF AGM saying 'People are counting on me.' False bravado. He should have been headed to the hospital.

Cody draws people to him like iron filings to a magnet. His CF Avengers has no age barriers. Pictured with Australian entertainment legend Kamahl.

Someone I love has CF.

Only years later, did I come to grips with the thought that we were all 'breathing through a straw'. Are you an organ donor yet? There is no greater gift, than the gift of *life!*

'I plan to get out of bed every day I am able to and do something good in the name of the donor family, who, in their most horrific hours, gave me another chance.' — Cody

CHAPTER 11

Cody's Incarcerations

Cody can gain incredible power from his worldwide cluster of friends. His 'cystas' and 'fibros' send up internet and social space smoke signals at all hours, and in all sorts of emotional and medical weather. When the news is good, he thrives; when it's bad he often has to muster hard, to pull himself out of the bowels of feeling bad. I can tell from a fairly good distance when his news is bad. His dawg, Texas often knows before me.

> *I'm sure you all have heard the news of Hope passing …*
> *This was quite a shock to us as a foundation. Hope was one of our biggest supporters and wasn't able to make it to this year's 5K due to being locked up. She had been in since April/May. She chose to stop all care yesterday and passed away today … Her daughter Courtney is without a mother and her family is without a daughter/cousin/aunt/niece …*

Hope was a special person and loved everyone she met. I had just talked to her a week ago when she went back in. We had sent her a care package because all she wanted was a coloring book and some crayons to pass the boredom. Hope, we will miss you greatly. ♥♥ ♥ *We love you.*

– postings like this, break me. I honestly don't know some days, how these CF kids put their feet on the floorboards …

Second home: hospital stays

I've started sending quirky, funny postcards to Cody's caregivers, 'thumpers' and physios, Doc Morton and the nurses on the children's ward. Wacky items that challenge the entire team. 'You MUST Read THIS Out Loud! … OR Fart!' I was happily surprised to discover that the nurses had saved each one and posted them openly for everyone to read. They dangle them on strings, so the kids can flip them over and see the picture on the front. Clever crew they are and I love them like family.

– Journal entry, Cape Town, 1999

As a kid, Cody spent at least eight weeks of each year in the hospital. Visits ran for two to three weeks at a clip and he made the most of his incarcerations with good humor. But they also frightened him greatly.

The children's hospital at Randwick in Sydney allowed parents and loved ones to sleep on the ward and set aside a unisex room with a half-dozen cots, and Cody never went a single night without having his parents or his Aunt Cathy, or one of his 'other mothers' on deck for a 'sleepover'. When his cousins Liz and Eloise got older, they too could stay over on the ward, toting along board games, smuggled-in goodies to munch, cards and other implements of entertainment. I walked into the playroom one evening after lights-out to find Cody's bed empty, among others, only to discover his cousins Eloise and Lizzie had commandeered the kids who could, creating a makeshift circus tent out of the laundered bed sheets, and had supplied flashlights to tell campfire stories underneath. There were also two of the nurses holed-up under there! The kids inhaled marshmallows, and I watched as one of the RNs sitting cross-legged next to my son slipped him his dose of enzyme tablets.

Despite the IV drips and the perpetual background of wonderful kids being horribly sick, everyone did their very best to make the most of the place. We shared the corners and corridors of happiness wherever we could find them. The fabulous Starlight Foundation created a room of the same name, populated most nights of the week by volunteer clowns and DJs via their very own sound booth and camera gear, dedicated DJs created their very own closed-circuit kids' program. Live. Many a time Cody, his brother Dylan, sister Hayley and cousins Eloise and Lizzie would ad lib segments, tell jokes or simply show their butt cracks to the camera to hampers full of laughter. Lots of other really sick kids who were bed bound could watch from their cots. For a couple of hours, a few nights every week, kids and parents could almost, forget where they were.

Cody and his CF pal Scotty still hold the overland record for covering the fifth-floor corridors in under 30 seconds while connected to IV drip poles on wheels. Not even the younger nurses could catch them. When I stayed, I toted along microwave popcorn and Cadbury chocolates (Cody'd let me know what supplies were 'needed') for the staff. Cody maintained a punchbowl full of goodies, which nested on the countertop of the nurses' station. I once stepped out of the elevator to witness Cody flying down the corridor atop his IV drip pole. He was being pulled along by another kid with cancer. The girl pulling him had no hair, but she wore a rainbow-colored Snoopy scarf, which flowed out behind her. On another occasion I arrived to see Cody's best buddy ever, his brother Dylan, racing him in a commandeered wheelchair. The nurses on the ward gave a wide laneway to those kids, and I loved them deeply for it.

Some days when our son was too unwell to get out of bed for the short walk to the Starlight room, an entire army of well-intentioned and equipped volunteers and a clown or two loaded down with donated toys and computer games would rock up at his bedside to add a bit of cheer. Even when he said it felt like there were nails sticking in him, he still managed to smile.

Extended family – stock owners and stakeholders in our Cody

'Dad! When you come in, can you get a cake. Jodi's birthday is today, and she just told the other nurses she's pulling a double shift. Don't do candles, 'cause we can't

*have matches. Bring balloons too, they have a pump in
the Starlight room I can use to blow them up ... I like the
chocolate ones, de-member?'*

– Journal entry, Cody age 12, 2001

Cody's caregivers were, and are still, remarkable people.
They have become wonderful additions to our extended
family. I may have said it before, but there is no way of
accounting for the gratitude I have for these people.
Cody and I for years now have been making Captain
America visits to various wards delivering, tidings of
thank you SOOOO much: sandwich presses, toaster
ovens, microwaves for the nurses' lounge and coffee
makers have found their way into St Vincent's, RPA, and
Westmead hospitals over the years. Cody and I usually
make a day of it. I love these occasions. They bring me,
and my son great joy. Even now, I try to never go along to
my GP or the pharmacy without bringing some fresh fruit
or chocolates, just to let these good people know we see
them.

A few years ago now, I started writing about our Cody
with the conviction that this wonderful kid, was a combined
effort of hundreds, if not thousands of fine people who could
easily lay claim to a piece of his progress. I suggested this
to his fabulous respiratory team and the nurses on the fifth
floor of Westmead Hospital on Cody's 25th birthday. Nurses
who had the day off came in to celebrate and eat cake.
When I said they all owned a piece of our kid, they jokingly
started prodding him and twisting his toes to determine
which might be the best bits of our boy to claim: the

innuendos were wonderful and Cody very seldom blushes with pride! These dedicated medicos, like hundreds of others in different parts of the planet, did their part to inspire, encourage and motivate Cody along his journey, and they have every right to claim collaborative ownership of *our* son. I love all of 'em.

Breaking-in new nurses!

I sit, smiling like a kid in anticipation of Santa's landing, and in awe of what's coming. A lovely new admitting nurse, clipboard in hand, pen at the ready, fully efficient, asks Cody to please outline the medications he's currently taking before he can be admitted. I settle into my chair, sit back and watch Cody go to work. My only regret was not having a coffee in my palm.

The admitting nurses often asked if Cody could repeat the frequency of dosages, and if he would kindly spell the name of the medications. At one time Cody took a phone snapshot of this list, which filled an entire page of the admissions form from top to bottom. Some of his meds, too many to find space, were written in the open margin spaces.

Sesame Street, Bananas in Pajamas, Don Spencer and the fabulous Mr Rogers

When you have kids, you start singing the theme songs to children's TV programs in your sleep. Honestly, for all the evil things television is meant to deliver to our youth, it equally saved us in similar measure. It held our hands and helped us hugely. While Cody-son was head down, towel across his chest and being rattled to break up the gunk threatening to suffocate him, we could hum along to 'The Crocodile Song' or a tall tale about the alphabet with Cookie Monster and Count Dracula on the tube. It eased us into the minimum two hours each day while doing our son's postural drainage. When Cody was in the hospital for long periods of time, this task would be undertaken by a physio staff member or a nurse. For me, they were never as good as the thumps he was delivered by his mother. I could see the dedication with every pat on his chest or back his mom administered. Cody liked lots of his physio-thumping troops.

I'd sit, mostly bored, when watching Mr Rogers with the kids. At home we three 'men' (Cody, Dylan and me) piled atop the massive blue beanbag to watch. I would often nod off for a wee nap, but the boys would be fully engaged and captivated by Mr Rogers. I think it's something in his constant and melodic tone that, like the Pied Piper, lures small children into his living room. I'm grateful for television; it gives me a chance to snuggle up to the kids and catch a few winks at the same time.

All hands in the cookie jar

This is more than a metaphor. We have a real tin cookie jar around this place, and it catches every spare coin I have in my pockets. In Australia this adds up! The kids know it's there and tap into it from time to time. When its overflowing, we sit around the table, counting. And the funds get used, always targeted on something we can do as a family. At times this amounts to hundreds of dollars in folding dosh, and we contemplate how best to use it. Mad money sometimes, to lock in something that one of kids need or the family might use. Theatre tickets, concerts, our new TV, Nintendo stuff, floaties for a beach visit, sometimes even the sweet suite at a weekend farm stay. Even as the kids moved along and became independent, they knew there was always something in the cookie jar for them, loose change, planted there with love. There, still is. One year, I gifted Hayley with that year's tin box, loaded to the top with one- and two-dollar gold coins I'd collected. A few months later, Dylan and I were toting some furniture for her to her mom's place and Dylan, spotting the tin, was automatically drawn to it, lifting the top to see what he was good to go for! From time to time, I'll gift the tin, fully loaded, to the kids and replace it with another, always the same, so we all know how to find it. It's not how much you earn, it's how much you get to keep. And how you spend it. Bridget and I never cut corners on the important things for our kids. Once, when we'd made the financially hefty decision to buy a not-yet-subsidized medication, Bridget jokingly said, 'We'll just eat a lot of spag bol and hot dogs!'. Pleasing priorities!

I'm talkin' here! – Cody-son

My mom, noting my infatuation with the doctors and nurses who scurried around the ward with a stethoscope around their necks, bought me one. It turns out it was a Rolls Royce version (Littman), better than the stock inventory type that appear kicking about on the back of nursing station chairs or draped over a drip pole. And I'd strut the halls or visit the Starlight room with my scope draped over my neck like a mink and wondered how hard it would be for a CF kid to actually make it through medical school; most of us were not expected to live long enough.

The coolest part of having the 'industry-best' scope on the ward was my sweet-as nursing pals would often ask if they could try it on. Even Doc Morton, my bowtie wearing CF specialist had a go. One day my dad, who wears bow ties as well, wore his Harvard tie to the ward, and Doc Morton said he'd also spent some time at the medical school there in Cambridge, but sadly, never had the time during his high-speed tenure to collect a tie with the Latin and crimson inscription of a Harvard man. My dad undid his collar and they swapped ties on the spot, and many years later at the memorial service for Doc Morton, his widow kindly remembered the gesture and the tie as one of her husband's best. My dad and I both cried and stood at the back of the service in the sun, pretending it was the sun's glare that caused our eyes to water. My entire life, good solid and smart people have been helping keep me healthy; Doc Morton, was without question, one of the very best of them.

– Cody

Not-so-trivial CF trivia

During one admission in 1996, Cody's nice niece Lizzie gifted him a hand-me-down calculator. He'd commented before his admission that it looked like an item that his hero James Bond as 007 might have tucked up into his tuxedo. Lizzie remembered this, and when her mom brought her for a kids' ward visit, presented it to him. She knew he'd love it to bits.

Our children's cousins are remarkably close and loving. They share a massive network of genuine caring among themselves which has extended into their adulthoods. Family gatherings are always like energy drinks for me. For the fun of it, Lizzie and Cody played a game of numbers about Cody's medications.

Cody takes about 30 pancreatic enzyme tablets each and every day of his life, which equates to 210 a week, or a whopping 10,920 a year. At the time of Lizzie's gift, Cody had just turned nine so that meant he'd swallowed 98,280 of the pills required to explode in his gut, to assist him in the digestion of his food. If you want to extrapolate even further, each tablet contains 100 tiny time bombs. That's give or take 9,820,000 tiny little beads that blow up in a CF kid's belly. At the age of 27, Cody had ingested over two million of the little darlings, or about 680 kilos of tiny, tiny depth charges that explode in his CF gut. That kind of ongoing dumping ground wreaks lethal havoc with any digestive tract, which goes a long way to explaining the pain, and inevitable damage to the spleen, the pancreas, the liver and the kidneys.

As a sidenote, I must confess, Cody has become so very adept at doing this, I even forget he has to take them. Even *after* a successful triple-organ transplant, Cody still swallows 'em. The message on my new T-shirt reads, 'Someone I LOVE has CF'.

No capsules? No Cody!

The upside is that Cody can, eat the foods he loves and the pills are a small part of keeping him well. When he gets the levels wrong, its hell to pay at the toilet. Over the years, Cody's enzyme intake caused serious damage to his liver, spleen and other interior parts. The pills are a mixed blessing but one we're grateful for.

Cody's enzyme tablets work a lot like the depth charges used to hunt down submarines. They get launched into the patient, and then at a suitable depth the capsules dissolve, sending thousands of break-down enzymes into the digestive tract, helping digestion. More importantly, they allow the food's nutriments to be absorbed, instead of simply having food come out the other end of a CF kid in pretty much the same condition as when it went in.

Sometimes friends-for-life is a hard pill to swallow

When Cody was a whippersnapper, his best pal 'forever' was Jasper, who was often either at our home, or Cody at his. His parents were Cody's parents, and likewise, when Jasper was in our care, he was a member of the Sheehan clan. The two young fellas were real partners, which meant that if one of them was into trouble, you could just about guarantee the other had a foot- or handhold on it as well.

Jasper was a smart and very inquisitive kid, and one afternoon, while I was dishing up grilled cheese sandwiches for the boys, Cody splayed out about a dozen pancreatic enzymes on the tabletop. There were no secrets between these two, and Jasper asked what the pills did. Cody explained in kid-speak that they helped him to digest his lunch, and I elaborated. Jasper then said, if they were good enough for his best buddy, they'd be good enough for him and he swallowed one, to show his support. Cody used to be very discreet when taking his enzymes, and after that, he was not at all shy about lining up his tablets when his closest pals came around to our home.

CHAPTER 12

'Boarding Passes, Please!'

Travel has the capacity to enlighten, inspire and motivate us – if the returns on this notion paid accordingly, I'd be a very wealthy fella indeed. Even when I didn't have to, I welcomed the chance to pick up, pack up and travel. In my adult lifetime, I'd have to say the trips Bridget planned were always the best. I'd object to some of the plans she had, but in my heart, I knew already what she'd suggested was going to be pure gold. Even the short weekends away were remarkable. Sometimes, because of treatments or needed procedures, our travels were confined to trips closer to home, which didn't require hopping on airplanes. Often the short breaks were the best ones.

Speakin' Zimbundi! Stay close ... travel far!

I'm not sure how Bridget discovered The Retreat at Wisemans Ferry, on the Hawkesbury River just north of

Sydney, but it was so fine, we took other friends along when we revisited on a few occasions. I love the notion of driving not too far from our front doorstep, and then parking the family wheels until we head for home again. The place had it all: tennis courts, fishing ponds, canoes, shuffle boards and badminton, a meal plan with lunch boxes tossed in, and we never turned the TV on once. Even short breaks had a positive impact on our family life; time spent together getting there and back, without the distraction of Game Boys, or in-cabin movies or any of other distractions from playing I Spy, With My Little Eye. Or creating our own language!

> *Tonight our waitress is a cute young junior school gal in year 10, who is astounded by Hayley's masterful control of Zimbundi. I peek over the menu, and ask my tiny Princess, nested in her booster chair, what she'd like to eat in her native tongue of Zimbundi, and she in turn smiles broadly and replies with 'Zaa zie, tootkumbas, na ways waie dadda.' Addling in English, 'Please father' at the end for good measure. Our waitress is in complete awe at my daughter's proficiency. Later, this young lass has assembled discreetly the entire white-aproned cook-staff at the porthole window of the kitchen, pointing a bedazzled finger towards our daughter. The cook, and dishwasher, salad guy and other waitresses all line up in turn for a look. I pretend not to see them there.*
>
> *The following morning, after we've repeated the sting again for bacon and eggs, our cutie reveals that she went home and told her parents about what a remarkable feat it must be, to achieve full fluency in another language, as she admitted struggles with basic*

English. Bridget just rolled her eyes at our deception,
and Cody and Dylan happily went along for the joy of it
all. I'm an American, and although the food plan in this
place included taxes, meals, and services, I'm leaving
a $20 bill on the table for the kid before heading for
home.

– Journal entry, Wisemans Ferry, NSW, 1995

Postcards from the other side

When Dylan's Montessori teacher, Lizzie (I love that Montessori platform, where the teacher you have in Year 1, is the very same teacher you have in Year 6!) said the class was doing geography through the year, I said I'd happily write postcards to the class from the places I was jetting to for my work. For an entire year, I addressed notes and postcards to the class, testing and tempting them to find me, like a *Where's Wally?* game. I added my boarding passes as well for the bragging rights, because so many of them had 'courtesy upgrades' stamped on them to first class. In those days, if there were an empty seat at the skinny end of the plane, I'd get it.

Bridget was again the 'class mother' for all our children and she toted my boarding passes along to class to pin on the massive National Geographic world map at the back of the room.

When I was invited at year's end to pop in and catch-up with Dylan and his class, I was stunned to see just how much of the globe my boarding passes covered. I balked, not knowing if I should be happy or saddened at the reality of it all. I'd been away from loved ones that long; gone that far astray from the ones I should have been home for. Suddenly I knew how my old man felt every Sunday when we all six kids took him to the airport with his leather-trimmed bag and he climbed aboard yet another plane to someplace else.

The Sun-Herald newspaper did a feature story that year about how Bridget and the kids helped to keep me connected. They sent round a photographer to capture a picture of us all, clad in bow ties on the front porch, and a collage of the kids' art and notes Bridget had hidden in my jockey shorts and socks. Across the rickety table I'd made before Cody was created, postcards to our kids I'd written in reply were splayed out. Some I'd planted as hidden treasure in the backyard, while others I wrote using hieroglyphics for the kids to translate. I started wearing a watch with two faces; the top time always helped me to put myself at home and was set on wherever Bridget and our kids were; the bottom clock pointed to the local time. On some trips, I was flying so fast, I'd put a piece of paper on the hotel carpet to remind me of the city I was in. Cape Town, Singapore, Kuala Lumpur, London, New York, Durban, San Francisco … sometimes I couldn't keep up, with trying to 'just keep up'. Run fast enough and avoid sinking in the pluff mud.

I look at my two-faced watch and I can time travel. It's Saturday morning at home (tomorrow!) and Bridget is on the sidelines at the soccer field. Dylan is running head-on defense, with a passion to protect his buddy Bowen in goals. Pretty Princess Hayley is sitting in her mother's lap, sharing a sausage sizzle …

– Journal entry, Port Elizabeth, South Africa

I'm pathetic with numbers, and can't seem to retain the simplest of facts like what I had for breakfast yesterday – even though I never eat breakfast, I still have to stop and ponder – but I can recount verbatim conversations that took place 25 years ago, and the weather, musical background, and even clothing colors the other folks in the recollection were wearing. When I was homesick, I'd simply rewind and play back a scene from the playroom at home: It's over 80 degrees, and Cody sports a pair of Batman underpants, topped off with a cowboy hat for balance. He strums a plastic guitar, one of his prized possessions, while singing along with Don Spencer's TV song about 'crockidyles' and penguins. His brother Dylan, also in Batman underpants and shirtless, sported a holster loaded with a white-handled cap-gun. Bridget's tied his 'blankie' around his neck as a cape.

Postage due! Better than phoning home!

I have a habit of making friends with our mailman. You can learn a great deal about your surroundings if you just linger a bit longer at the postbox and attach a six-pack of beer or a decent bottle of wine to it a few times a year around the holidays. You'll find out which of your neighbors is a 'bitch' and what pets are a pain in the prat, but you can also pick up bits you'd never even considered about your town.

The downside, if you can call it that, of my postcard habit is the fact that a postcard is by its very nature public disclosure. And I've been exposing myself for years and years now, without even thinking about it. Much like my notes in bottles, I've been launching missives for over 40 years and counting, and never really stopped to think about the ramifications or who the readers might be on the other end of the bottle. What I did learn from my creative postcards was they had an audience all their own. I'd fire off a treasure map for the kids, detailing how they could pace off and find a treasure chest I'd hidden in the backyard. I used my own hieroglyphics and images to do this that included childishly simple crayoned icons as footsteps, hearts, trees and even swing sets to provide the bearings for Hayley and the boys. My postman enlightened me one Easter lead-up that the entire post office staff was now on high alert to follow my planetary travels and see what I was saying to the kids. I also wrote provocative notes to beautiful Bridget about undressing her as soon as I made my way home, or updates on my shopping spree for me (her!) at Victoria's Secret. Apparently, with the postal service, nothing is sacred as long as it lives on the outside of the envelope!

> I spent an entire week, sleeping in the most-haunted hotel rooms in America; and let me tell you, they are not very close to one another!
>
> The state fellas who attempt to boost visitation gave me free rein of massive, leather-lined rental cars, enough gas to get me to places without having enough fuel to ever get me back to the airport depot, and an 88-page Rand McNally road map the size of a poster. I had letters of introduction in my top pocket, No-Doz to keep me alert on the long road trips and flights in-between haunted beds and, maybe, to keep me alert enough to see the nocturnal ghosts who'd been notified of my arrival dates.

*I did hear noises at night when I was in room 301
at the Calumet Inn in Minnesota; the young couple
next door from Wisconsin were enjoying a second
honeymoon. I only learned this over a buffet breakfast,
but judging from the decibel levels between the old walls,
I don't think they ever really enjoyed a first honeymoon.*

*Some of the other ghostly noises I'd encountered
are not suitable for mention, as many of them were
omitted from my midriff after the most tear-jerking
Midwestern curry I've ever encountered; they say
Chicago is the home of the most spice-riddled pizza
on the planet, but let me tell you, the curry in Red Wing
Minnesota makes the Chicago pizza melt like buttermilk
in your mouth. Red Wing is also the home of the biggest
boot in the world!*

*Cody called me on my mobile, wanting to spare
me a text message which he* **knew**, *would send me
into emotional overdrive. Hearing his voice, and his*
promise, *to still be okay when I did arrive home, helped.
But I'm a worrier by nature, and even with all my stars
aligned, it took me over three whole days to get to the
front doorstep. Cody had called from his hospital bed –
bleeding lungs.*

– Journal entry, Minnesota, 2015

Until I started to leave home myself, I never fully understood why our father hated leaving

Our father spent a good bit of his professional life in hotel rooms, board rooms and at 35,000 feet. Both Pan Am and United Airlines awarded him VIP status, long before frequent fliers and mileage rewards were even invented. I still have the gold bag-tags (and gold life member's card from the New York Athletic Club) with his name engraved on them.

I recall one summer, our mother had the hardware store deliver an entire truckload of timber, nails and fixings onto our driveway. She challenged my older siblings to make a plan, measure, cut and complete a roofed-in back porch before our father flew home on the Friday. We all got involved, power tools, hand saws and hammers akimbo and I planted my tiny pawprints in the concrete alongside my siblings. We'd built with great gusto and painted, guttered and roofed an entire back porch on our home. I puffed up with incredible pride; I was just mirroring the emotions of my brothers and sisters who'd played a part.

When our father returned on the Friday afternoon, I could not understand why, when he saw our accomplishment, he was suddenly so very saddened. He did a double-take, mumbled something about having a headache. He picked up his bag and retreated indoors. It was so very out of character for him.

Now I understand. I get it: like me, my father wanted everything to stay as it was, frozen in time for his return. He had also been 'left out' of a major family event, which I now know, truly broke his heart.

On other occasions, our mother would soften his re-entry by reporting newly installed casts and crutches before our father came home. I get it now.

Just before my mother died, I asked her about our father. He and I hadn't spoken for the last three months of his life, and I know it caused him tremendous pain. My mother's reply stunned me when she said: 'Your father was the best husband I could have ever asked to be gifted! He was smart, and creative and when he was home, he was totally and fully here with us all. He was a fabulous provider of affection to both his wife and all his children. Other fathers might "commute" and be home for meals each day, but your father never once opened the newspaper at the dinner table or asked me to put his dinner on the table after you'd all been put to bed. After dinner he was there with his kids, scrubbing the copper-bottomed pots. Your father was forced to leave home for work, and he found "distractions" to make it bearable. And he led me a merry chase, but he was a remarkable man and an exceptional father.'

I only wish I'd asked her while he was still around.

Bridget did everything possible to keep me connected. She had become for me, like my mother before her, my religion.

Some trips were, much harder than others

I'd speak with Bridget at length sometimes, hearing about how it went with the visit to bow-tied Doc Morton, and a summary which included a failing lung function, or the need to pull Cody yet again from his loved classroom teacher and pals for a readmission to the hospital. When I had my turn with the boys on the phone, Cody would tell me he was doing just fine, but Dylan, Cody's perpetual wingman, would ask the question Cody was always keen to ask: 'Dad, when are you coming home?' These calls could devastate me for days, knowing that if I kept to my appointed rounds, I'd not see my family for another pair of weeks or more.

Once, before I purchased my two-faced watch, I called Bridget to wish her good luck with the school play; she reminded me in a sleepy voice that everything at home was fine (she was whispering at the time, a child spooning alongside her) and that it was *not* three in the afternoon, but 3 am, dummy. The 'dummy' part was delivered with kindness and understanding. I bad.

When I was home, I vowed to spend as much time around the kids and Bridget as possible. I'd paint a bedroom, plant grass, build a fence, take the kids to the playground down the laneway, and mostly just be underfoot. I loved taking the kids to school and picking them up and offered and enjoyed doing the grocery shopping so Bridget could relieve some of the solo pressures she had while I was away. If I were home for eight weeks or more, Bridget might jokingly say, 'When are you taking off again?!' It was usually, after the kids and I had turned the playroom into a fort, upturning the furniture and using all the freshly cleaned bed linens to create Bedouin tents in the backyard. I know she was only jesting, but I would rehash my options for quitting my job, and maybe trying my hand at buying a bakery. I love getting up very early, even on mornings when I don't have to.

I tried to make Sundays special. I, with the help of the kids, might make Bridget breakfast in bed, or slip out to buy croissants and the Sunday paper, knowing Bridget loved her bed and could live there if she had the option on Sundays. This was a practice I enjoyed, long before Bridget and I ever married or started our clan.

I detest getting on that plane today. Cody-son is due for a visit to Doc Morton, but I already know what it means. Bridget and I could hear him coughing through the double-brick walls. I'll be unable to sleep on the flight, so I'll just keep ordering alcohol, knowing my family is on the ground behind me. Needles in my son, plastic, child-sized-masks loaded with toxic-smelling meds vaporising out of the small portholes with every exhale. My feeling of hopelessness; unable to help with anything but dollars while my wife and son have nowhere to escape. Drunk at 35,000 feet and counting. I detest getting on that plane today.

Journal entry, Sydney to San Francisco United
upgrade, 1993

Fear of flying. And sleeping … and waking …

I'm in a palatial poolside suite at the Marriott in Los Angeles; the manager's placed a gift basket on the coffee table with a bottle of Napa Valley wine, and nibbles. I'm jet lagged, sleepless and hungover all in the one package. At check-in, the lovely lass behind the desk lets me know I have a complimentary $100 gift voucher, to use in the hotel at any venue that pleases me. Including the sports bar and Victoria's Secret.

After my shower, I discover a cute piece of kid's art in my clean socks, tucked in there by Bridget; my wife often puts pieces of herself or the kids in among my luggage, which reveal themselves as I travel. This helps to keep me connected to the ones I love back home. I sift through my other gear, desperate for further connections to my loved ones and find four more notes from my wife, melded with some kid's art. I replace the treasure back into the underpants and socks, so I can rediscover them all again when I'm in another city. I was away from home for three weeks again that time. Torture for me. When Bridget and I made a pact in our Charleston kitchen to do whatever we had to, my wife got the harder end of the bargain. We said we'd wait until Cody got to 21, and then, balance the books. I had the easy part: I only need to make the money, which for me had always been more of a hobby. Bridget locked up her dreams, aspirations and career path with a massive chain. In 21 years, I could count on 10 fingers the number of days Bridget took off to do something for herself. Meanwhile, I was being given seats at the front of the plane to leave her and my family behind.

I would often think about the possibility of successfully robbing a bank, so I could end the travel and stay home. Only the prospect of being caught and locked away from my loved ones prevented me from considering this line of work seriously.

Lake Tahoe and the slippery slopes of Rubicon

Cody and Dylan set up their kid-sized beach chairs ($4 each at Walmart in Reno, Nevada) on our porch overlooking Lake Tahoe. It was our second night in our new Tahoe home. They'd arrived from Oz on the 4th of July, jaws dropped as they watched the fireworks from our new balcony. I'd told them the fabulous fireworks display was a welcome celebration just for them. So, the next night they were camped out, expecting the same again. After all it was a three-day, long-weekend celebration.

I've spent the majority of my married, professional life, with two exceptions, in and around tourism and travel. Bridget has allowed me to roll the dice in this arena on more occasions than I might have asked. Bridget always felt that at least if I was going to gamble everything, it was on a game I was most familiar with. She happily toted our kids, packed and unpacked homes in all four corners of the globe and saw every endeavor with the true spirit of a real partner and adventurer. I thank my stars daily for her, and our three children, who also appear to have inherited this same get-up-and-go enthusiasm for the new and often unknown trail.

But it was a massive stretch for my entire family, when I said I wanted to quit my gravy-train position in Australia, for the outsider's chance of entering the cut-throat and highly competitive garment industry back in the USA. For perhaps the first time in 15 years of married life, I think my spouse considered having me 'looked at' by a professional. The carrot was dangled when a new brand startup, later to be known as Rubicon Sports was in its infancy in Lake Tahoe and I was asked to come aboard as the sales and marketing director. With a pretty piece of the company, stock options and other seductions tossed in.

I argued the clean air and water could be good for our kids. Lake Tahoe sits at 7000 feet (2100 metres) above sea level, and you can scoop the pure water out of the lake to drink in your hand. It's 99.9 per cent pure snowmelt. We had to give our kids fluoride tablets because the beautiful water was untreated. And Rubicon Sports was on the 'income-free' side of the lake. Our new home on Country Club Drive was exactly in the right place according to our accountant.

In the entire time we spent in Tahoe, Cody was not hospitalized once. I figure it was because the air was clean, and his lungs had to, unknowingly, work harder all the time to enjoy it. Cody had no idea he was toughening up his lungs, and fighting to breathe, even when he was sleeping or watching his favorite TV program alongside his brother.

The full Rubicon story is for the telling another time, but it showed me one thing I'd always suspected but was never fully able to confirm until I took the challenge of changing industries 'cold turkey'. I had an immense learning curve to cut through, but I also had an entire arsenal of weapons at my fingertips that had never been applied in the rag trade. I might have been an outsider, but I quickly discovered I had the inside edge on the folks who'd been plodding along the 'traditional' tracks to success in this field. I was, again, away from home a lot, leaving Bridget and the kids behind. Bridget contracted a guy with a massive snowplough to clear our 100-yard-long driveway. Lake Tahoe gets about 15–20 feet (about 5–6 metres) of snow-dump each winter, and the lake is 3000 feet deep (900 metres), and it is always, always cold! I hate the cold weather.

Covertly, there were two big lures for me to be making the move. The first was, that I didn't have to get on an airplane and travel internationally for weeks on end, leaving my loved ones. The second lure was all about the money if my partners were committed to the notion of an initial public offering. I'd always wanted to try my hand at an IPO on the Nasdaq. Rubicon Sports and my new partners promised we'd reach for the stars. I was keen to reach along with them.

Rubicon rules and we got season-long passes!

Our Rubicon gear had a real reputation. *SKI* magazine said we created 'bombproof parkas' and 'Sherman tanks with zippers', and before long Rubicon was providing uniforms for 90 per cent of the Tahoe-area ski resorts. And we got free all-season lift passes. As a PR, marketing and sales fella, I could sell the stuff with passion, but I didn't have a clue how to stay on a ski lift, snowplough or get from the top to the bottom of the nursery slopes without breaking a new crack in my ass.

Plus, I hate the cold; always have, but when in Rome, do as the Venetians.

The boys take ski lessons and I emulate from behind the glass

I enrolled the boys in ski lessons, and they took to it like bass to bait. They were already low to the ground when they fell. I'm 6"1' and weigh in easily at over 200 pounds (90 kilograms) these days. I sat on the nursery slope and eavesdropped on every one of the boys' lessons.

I knew nothing, nada, zip. Yet I was one of the 'boys from Rubicon!' sporting the gear of the pros. Expectations ran high and I did my best. My brother David and his family came for a visit, and he quietly took me aside on day one, and gave me a few tips, which saved my life and got me started. He was very discreet.

Cody is a skilled technique skier, making wonderfully wide and controlled turns on any slope. Dylan is the complete opposite, more of a Kamikaze kid on skis and a snowboard. Dylan heads straight down the hill crouched like a small bulldog. I was compelled to get them helmets.

The week I 'learned to ski', Sonny Bono of Sonny and Cher fame ran into a tree on the very same mountain, killing himself. He was the Mayor of Palm Springs at the time, where the temperature was idling around 75 degrees in the shade.

Dad! Hayley was airlifted by helicopter and it's on the evening news!

The thing about families who have a loved one with a chronic, life-threatening illness is that on top of the everyday challenges, life goes on. Other kids fall off swing-sets, get the flu, need a stitch or two and skin knees. The mortality rate for marriages is far higher for partnerships who are confronted with the never-ending challenges of chronic illness. Coping as a married couple is tough: I was lucky that my partner was strong enough, resilient enough to push ahead. In American grid-iron 'football', when you have a 'guard' plowing towards the goal line, you tuck the football in close, put yourself behind them, and just follow their lead. My partner cut the way for us through the enemy lines, all I had to do was run forward in her wake. The majority of CF marriages melt.

I was on my very last writing trip to the USA, sponsored by the state of Nevada and Destination America, when I got a call at 3 am from Dylan saying: 'Don't worry Dad, they think Hayley's going to be able to walk just fine, but she'd like to have you here if you can make it. She's been asking for you.'

From the time I got the call, until I could arrange flights, and cancellations, and with frantic calls texts and email messages, it was over 25 hours to get to her hospital bedside.

The very same day as Hayley's accident, Cody, who'd gone to the clinic with Bridget for a routine review had also been admitted to the hospital for an inflamed and infected spleen and complications. Nobody was going to recall me for his readmission, knowing it would only upset me, and I'd be unable to do anything about it from such a distance. Cody's hospital bed was separated from his sister's by about 40 kilometres. Two out of three of our children in 'the slammer', and me, thirty hours off and fly-fishing. With a private fishing guide.

Thankfully, I've got great sisters, Bridget, and an extended family whom I was assured were filling in there while I was trying to get home. With such distances to cover, nothing happens swiftly. I threw money at it and refused to take no-can-do/no seats/sold out as a reply. Get me home. Please, *please*, was my mantra, delivered with tears rolling down my face.

Hayley was hit in broad daylight while crossing the road and had to be airlifted to the hospital. She now has a rod in her leg that's there forever, no doubt setting off airport security with each new airport adventure she takes. She made the evening news, and only eight weeks afterwards was walking about without crutches or a 'boot' and only sporting a few small scars.

When Hayley turned 21, I asked her if the steel rod ever hurt. She hugged me and said softly, *'Every* day.'

Hayley's now got a tattoo or two, ignoring my attempts to bribe her with cash offers to consider the removable ones. She's as headstrong as her father.

CHAPTER 13

September 11, 2001 – Walking Dead

I watched the planes fly into the side of the World Trade Center over and over in my head. Some bastard at NBC ran the footage then reversed it and ran it again in the event the viewers missed the shattering of glass and steel, and screams and horrors that must have followed. I replayed those few seconds over, and over, and over in my head, almost wishing my heart could not take it. After the shocking horror of September 11 and the cowardly terrorist attacks on America I had a toss-in-the-towel feeling of helplessness. I didn't feel much like doing anything at all. And I was mourning among millions. My heroes numbered in the thousands, as my own hometown of Manhasset, Long Island mourned for over 87 breadwinners who would never again catch the 7.22 train from Plandome Station to the big apple of New York City.

I kept playing the horrific footage of that second plane, gliding silently into the side of the World Trade Center over and over again with the same cadence that I'd used many years earlier to bounce a ball against a wall. We lost beautiful people on that day and again it was the smiles of my children and Bridget that drew me back. I had loved ones under my roof who were counting on me. I picked myself up and started wearing the mothballed sterling cufflinks my father made for each of his sons shortly before he died. They were simply etched with the letters YCDBSYA: 'You Can't Do Better Sitting on Your Ass'.

I took the call from Eric, about my death

Six weeks after the World Trade Center nightmare I was back in my family home on Long Island, New York. My hometown of Manhasset was doing weekly memorial services, having the highest losses on the day. The entire town was wearing black armbands and appeared to be in shock. While passing through to England, Scotland and Wales I attended three memorial services.

I'd just hung up the phone with Bridget, she in turn giving the phone to our sons so I could hear their voices; I'd been away for two weeks and counting, and I sat at my brother's desk afterwards to quietly cry. In my morning search for clean socks, I'd found the kid-art from our sons, Bridget had hidden there.

When the phone rang, I answered assuming it was Bridget ringing back, with some up-tempo news to cheer me. She could hear my sadness, being so far away. On the other end of the line was my childhood pal, Ricky Gibson, a doctor who had just seen the World Trade Center 'missing and presumed dead' list. My name was on it and he was calling to give his condolences to my family.

Because my offices for Destination America were both in New York and Los Angeles, I kept a daily 'room allocation' for myself in the World Trade Center Marriott Hotel. This assured me I'd have a room, even when city-wide conventions gobbled up hotel rooms like Pac-Man. I was living out of a suitcase and knowing before going that I had a bed set aside was at least one item I didn't have to consider when headed to Manhattan. The hotel list of registered guests on September 11 had my name on it.

It took me months afterwards to convince the powers-that-be that reports of my death had been significantly exaggerated. My kid brother Chris said, 'Just take the insurance money and start over; how many of us ever get that chance!' I actually thought about it for a time. I could, just possibly, stop the world and get off …

America First! And the aftermath …

When Cody was diagnosed, and I began to understand my delivery of a genetic death sentence to our first-born, I just wanted to give up. I would curl up with Bridget in our bed, Cody nested between us, pull the covers, and never get up. I was beyond any repair, completely emotionally disabled. Bridget saved me. She possessed a crystal ball which envisioned our son happy, in his teens and beyond, and she quietly shared it.

Again, when I replayed the World Trade Center horror in my head I felt hopeless. Even months later the images haunted and taunted me. Travel and tourism were in the toilet, and many of my peers and pals were hemorrhaging. We all face tragedy in our own way, and in the aftermath of September 11 I found a way to strike back. With heaps of help, we retaliated, and created the non-profit America First Campaign, and enrolled the support of American icons like Disney, Universal Studios, the states of California and New York and a dozen other outfits who were keen to retaliate after the World Trade Center attacks. In the two years we rolled out the campaign, I did seminars in 11 countries, and 'certified' over 8000 travel professionals. Creating America First put fresh air in my lungs, and although it took me away from my loved ones, it gave me a good reason to put my feet on the floorboards again.

I left home for weeks and months on end. Bridget never baulked even once. She was 24/7, 365 every day on deck while I darted around the planet. Money poured in from everywhere to support the campaign. I simply asked for help saying we needed a fire-starter for American tourism. Kickstarter kindling wood is needed to make a bonfire. We poured petrol on it. While Bridget continued to hold the home front and our family together, I charged ahead, a man with a mission to sell the United States with confidence to any audience that might listen.

Years later I was asked to 'cease and desist' the use of *our* America First Campaign by a political group, who'd adopted it for a presidential campaign slogan. I detested the candidate, whom I knew from my teens. Our refusal, and reply was brief! And, as a matter of decorum, not to be repeated in front of small children: imagine, a note on our America First Campaign letterhead, with just one, single, middle finger showing …

Stop the world I want to get off

For a parent with a CF child, you can't simply 'stop the world, I want to get off'. Globally things happen, and in our own backyards tragedies and seemingly monumental events occur. As a kid, whenever I had a fever and was ill, I had the same recurring nightmare. It's followed me into adulthood. I dream I'm running from something unseen, with a gigantic Cheerio on my left shoulder. My feet seem stuck and sluggish and refuse to work. There's never a happy ending to this nightmare: I wake abruptly, soaked in a cold sweat every time. I can't save the whales, or make an impact on global warming, or famine relief, but I'll happily toss a tenner into the bucket for the good people who are working on making the planet a better place. Where the rubber meets the roadway for me now, is in the changes I *can* make, in my own backyard.

With our son Cody, we were fortunate enough to be able to shop around and buy, often at our own expense, the newest drugs and medications to keep him treading water, as we waited, and waited, and waited for a cure. Other CF families we came to know and love could not hold out long enough. In so many ways, it's all about the money. Pharmaceutical companies and research outfits expect massive paybacks for breakthroughs, stockholders expect profits and dividends, and government agencies balk at the millions of dollars it would take to underwrite them. It took, over five years of tossing money at, and banging on doors, lobbying to get Kalydeco approved for CF sufferers in Australia. Today, newer, even better medications hover in the wings while lawmakers and our public servants ponder the costs and return on investment. When we learned of new treatments and meds, we actively lunged for them, even if we didn't have the dollars. Cody's mom always presented the new information about medications and treatments and then she would ask if it was possible for us financially.

CHAPTER 14

Hard Times on the Homefront

For the very first time in his life, I saw in Cody's face the look. He looked at our faces, camouflaging his feelings, and then turned on me saying, 'Why me?'

I stood helpless. Dumbfounded – I had no answer. After all, Cody had done his part, and much, much more. He'd smiled and risen above all the demands made of him; wasn't that enough?' When was it going to stop?! There was no brave face left.

When Cody came home from the hospital this time, after being further plagued with diabetes, which occurs in about 90 per cent of CF kids who make it to adolescence, he took an emotional nosedive. The fact was, he was going to have to, from now till forever, jab himself with insulin, take pin-prick readings of his blood-sugar levels, and add yet another 'must' to his already four-hour-long daily routine. Another set of needles, more instructions, more prescriptions. And the kid was right – it was so completely, not fair.

Cody was now toting into his spotlessly clean bedroom an entire new arsenal of needles, testers, refrigerated insulins and skinny, pocket-sized books on how to deal with a 'hypo' and avoid the ugly bruises that would come from sticking himself with a needle four or five times a day.

Before our son was handed the news of his diabetes, Cody had hand-crafted a magnificent hardwood headboard and bed, with a finely matched set of bedside tables, which he populated and maintained with all the things that mattered to him. The room was an example of well-tuned spotlessness. The tidiest, room in the whole house. For the first time ever, our son started closing the door of his immaculately well-ordered and clean bedroom. When he did emerge, the vapors I inhaled from his lair took on the aroma of his mess-blessed-brother Dylan, across the hallway.

Instead of dialing up porn (he might have been doing this as well) Cody moved the mouse about, reading all manner of information about the CF, and diabetes: making the discovery that he was far from the normal guy who could do anything and be anything his parents, family and teachers led him to believe was possible. We'd lied to our boy. Cody learned that he had considerably less time to play and accomplish stuff according to the statistics. Captain America was not happy about the notion of an earlier 'check-out time' posted like the printed card on the inside of a California hotel door.

My folks went out of the way to make sure I was going to grow up as close to everyday as every other kid on the block. It was only many years later – maybe I'm 'thick' – that I began to look around and observe some small, some significant differences in my life in contrast to the other kids I played with on the jungle gym and in the pool ... none of those kids needed to swallow a half-dozen enzymes with poolside pizza, or spent hours a day getting thumped and coughing up ugly plugs of mucus.

– Cody

For the first time I could recall, Cody stopped flapping his hands with genuine pleasure when he got excited. He'd go weeks without his previously daily smiles. I found excuses to travel, without the guts to ask what was going on. This was my Cody, my precious Cody in a place I could not fix by throwing money at it, or picking up a phone and making a consultation happen, or even reaching out to his mother for help. I did what I'd come to do best for most of my life; I'd just run for cover if I couldn't fix it. And I took to drinking during the day, again. I bought a new 99-cent notebook and created the table of contents for a new book. The working title was 'The Underground Alcoholic's Handbook'. Within the first hour, I'd already set up a dozen chapters.

Nothing happens in a vacuum, and while Cody's story goes on, it's melded into countless others. The year we learned of his diabetes was a devastating year for me all around. My traditional response to bad news is like the response of Pavlov's dog to hearing a bell ring. If I'm unable to run away, I either bury pain inwardly, or lash out in the direction of anyone who happens to be within emotional striking distance. The biggest target for my toxic shrapnel was my wife, followed closely by anyone in my office. Even the jovial bearded motorbike mailman took a lashing and stopped lingering at my postbox to chat.

Both Cody and I have lifted our game now, with loving help from Bridget, Dylan and Hayley. We've also had sincere help from the team at Prince of Wales Children's Hospital in Sydney, who've called us at home, chased us to be sure we were comfy with the procedures and, in general walked alongside us through yet another step in the process of kicking this cystic fibrosis thing in the shins. Like Cody, Bridget and I have also discovered an 'extended family' of caregiving and kinship at the children's hospital in Randwick. Dig deep when asked. The people who get out of bed every day, to help us beat this thing, do so quietly. Let them know you appreciate everything they do for us all.

Our Cody slumped for a time, then pulled himself up. He was surrounded by people who loved him, and if he was feeling sorry for himself, he never once outwardly showed it. Cody rapidly rearranged his priorities.

His tidy room could go to hell in the hamper (oddly, our kids' clothing never made it there – why bother, when the floor is fully carpeted!). Months earlier, Dylan hung a significant 'Do Not Enter' sign on his door, which must have been seen as an inspired message from God for our very Christian housekeeper. Cody followed his wonderful brother's lead with a skull and crossbones sign, supported by a ribbon of bright yellow crime-scene tape. Hayley hung a door sash I'd swiped from a hotel in the Catskills that said 'Shhhh hibernating!'.

Our son no longer yelped if I misplaced something on his bookshelf: none of that seemed to matter much. I was no longer openly welcome to just waltz into his room, but oddly enough, even among the outward apparent chaos of his space, Cody knew where everything was. He could direct me by phone with exacting clarity to a document he was hunting. Even to this day, Cody can need a document for the doctors and walk me to the fifth admission yellow copy of his discharge buried in the bowels of a pile of papers and folders, and then, in the same call, lead me like a prospector with mule, to the exact treasure chest where I'd unearth his needed medicine.

Sometimes Cody'd take longer, having to catch his wheeze, or a cough in mid-call. 'And don't forget Dad, I'd like you to bring the socks (not in the sock drawer!) which were a gift from my "cysta" in Ohio – the ones with the silly Santa on the sides.' Slight break in the conversation as I hear him drivel a plug of celery-green sputum into a specimen jar for Emily, his pretty nurse … 'You'll need the little stepladder at the foot of my bed old man to get 'em.'

Instead of doubling over emotionally, Cody straightened himself up, regrouped, and refocused. He decided to make a CF movie. He wanted to sing to an audience bigger than his home-team choir about what CF means to real people. Try walking and breathing in a CFer's shoes. Just breathe! Our son lobbied with us to enroll him in a filmmaker's course at NIDA (Australia's National Institute of Dramatic Arts) sweet-talked the Make-A-Wish Foundation to nail down a camera, tripod and editing goodies, wrote a script, did the casting, and read a book about how Steven Spielberg got started. Ya just had to love the kid. He made two films before he discovered ...

Cody also gave his mother and me permission to step back

When Cody turned 14 in 2013, he was asked to give a talk at a black-tie event at the Four Seasons Hotel in Sydney. I got my $99 off-the-rack tux out of its plastic condom for the event, and we went shopping for Cody's suit. His mom significantly sewed in the waistline as there was not much of him to fill it. The jacket drooped and hung on his long, slender torso, but I only saw Cody, my son, as the heavyweight prize-fighter when he stepped up to the stage to speak.

On the night, 800 well-heeled stockbrokers and their better, totally decked-out halves rocked up for the red-carpet event. Cody took the stage and began telling his story, complete with all his daily machinations, and asking for help. He owned his audience. Cody only stopped short on two occasions, to clear the glue-like gunk discreetly into his monogrammed handkerchief. It was a gift from his godfather, Shane, intended to bring him good luck.

He was Cody William Sheehan and he was the guy with the hand on his destiny now. Not a single dry eye in the house, including mine. I stood at the back, tears pouring down my face. A nearby waiter stopped in his tracks with a bottle of champagne and kindly handed over his handkerchief.

Although Cody's story was hard to hear, it was filled with hope and determination, and the power to move us all to a better future. His chat rattled our heartstrings and rang cash registers for the Cystic Fibrosis Foundation. The power of one, his crackling voice, reached out to everyone in the room. He went into the hospital the following day, exhausted and out of breath, with a smile on his face. I love this kid. He was in there for three weeks.

Black-tie events – annual outings

Saying 'thank you' packs a powerful punch, especially when it is said in a room full of wonderful people, all with a common cause. Let 'CF' stand for Cure Found! My tux jacket no longer closes with ease from the years of fun and fundraising events for cystic fibrosis. Oh yeah, and the adjustable pants with the silk strip down the sides stopped 'adjusting' when the zipper broke mid-chat from the podium. New clothes can be bought, old ones tailored to fit changing waistlines, but the cure for CF still evades us.

Meanwhile back at the ranch ...

Hayley's best friend's parents were openly in a downward spiral that was painful to us all. Their struggle was very much out in the open, and Bridget did her best as a go-between for our friends, while I stood furious and angry with these 'grown-ups', as they polluted my family homefront with their venom for each other.

> Hayley came home from school and I asked her what she'd learned today. She burrowed her head in her

chin and went quiet. I could see the small teardrops on the floor. My princess said she cried all through lunch, wrapped cocoon-like in the arms of her best-ever-ever friend 'B', and her teacher. B's family was a big part of our extended family, and the news was devastating. Hayley'd learned that the other couple were fighting real bad now, non-stop, and said they fucking hated each other. She made me promise that her mom and I would never ever get a divorce.

– Journal entry

Gotta problem? Throw money at it!

One of the very best networking people I know is Elizabeth Crundell. The lass could extract money from your wallet, while having you dig around for additional loose change to add to it. When she said we were going to raise a million bucks for the Children's Hospital in a single night, I raised my hand as a member of her board. I just wanted to watch and learn how she intended to do it. She had me embed the samurai battle creed of 'Learn the way of many weapons' in my head. We'd host a party in a massive tent and get all the grog and food and 'help' for free by enlisting volunteers for everything. We'd pick a date as close to the end of the financial year as possible and then go to all the corporate bigwigs, asking them to bring their wide-open checkbooks, knowing beforehand how much the corporate bean counter said they had to spend in 'donations' instead of taxes. Elizabeth conjured up fabulous live auction prizes and got me to arrange a five-night package in New York City with Broadway play tickets. The value of the prize idled around $5000.

On the night of the event, Elizabeth called me to the stage to describe the prize package and for impact I said clearly, the package was worth a whopping five grand. The very first bid was for $10,000 from the table of an iconic electronics company, followed by a bid from their biggest competitors on a table across the way for $20,000. I repeated for the crowd's pleasure, the value of the prize and it went onwards and upwards from there. When the bidding was done, the corporate winner said he was pleased to pay up and tossed the package back on the table. He challenged the 'other bastard' to do the same. Boom!

For years since then I've been involved in raising money and public awareness for finding a cure and other campaigns. Instead of fearing someone might say no to chipping in, focus on the satisfaction of telling someone else what you'd like to do with their money. Share the dream and offer hope. If you don't ask, you don't get.

The CF Avengers!

Cody started asking me how much it would cost to buy, say 25 toasters and sandwich presses for the hospital. Or send a box of chocolates and a care bear to the USA for a 'cysta' in the hospital who needed cheering-up. This was the start, without our even knowing it, of Cody's CF Avengers.

Cody would later adopt the notion of his heroes as 'mutants': after all, CF was a mutant gene, so he had a shared connection with comic legends like Captain America, the Hulk and others who were genetically altered from the 'norm'. When he was old enough to come under the microscope of Marvel Comics' scrutiny for misuse of the

Captain America persona, we approached the franchise's lawyers to admit guilt, telling them how Cody'd used the shield and Captain America's powers for finding a cure alongside his social media 'cystas' and 'fibros' in the creation of The CF Avengers. Cody's cystic fibrosis friends would nominate themselves, each picking a different mutant persona for approval, or Cody, acting as Captain America, would nominate one for them, depending on which traits fit each one best. Instead of the lawyers demanding a 'cease and desist' claim, they congratulated our son and said his timing was perfect, as the worldwide franchise was looking for a good cause to support. Full steam ahead they suggested, and outfits, authentic shields and other Marvel Comics props started landing on our doorstep. The power of positive energy emanated from a kid who'd just been told he didn't have too much longer unless ...

CHAPTER 15

Cody's Creative Cooking and Other Pursuits

Cody took a barista's certificate course, and a job with George Clooney. He demonstrated the art of making coffee from a metal capsule, and I was pleased because we got the state-of-the-art machine at home. The cupboards ran over with long tubes of java, none of which could be differentiated from the other without a score card.

One day, when I topped up my third cup of hand-twitching-already coffee with boiling water from the kettle, I noticed something different, a clanging of sorts in the kettle, and vowed to return later to investigate. When I did, I discovered a collection of nebulizer parts and pieces floating. It seemed that Cody had made the discovery that he could just dump the plastic parts into the hopper and do the whole bunch in one dipping. A time-saving innovation.

I started running-the-numbers in my head about the time Bridget, I and others would have spent every day, sanitizing stuff. With a half-hour for each of his two daily postural drainages and proper disposal of phlegm-filled plastic cups and tissues, I guessed making sure we kept it clean amounted to another hour and a half each and every day. Sitting in the doctor's reception, I'd often play with 'Cody calculations' and numbers on my pocket calculator. If it took us 10.5 hours a week to sanitize Cody's nebulizer mouthpieces, that translated to about 546 hours every year dedicated to doing just one of the extra bits it took to stay on top of germs and potential infections. If you backed that up, say, based on a 38-hour work week, every year we'd spent the equivalent of 14.38 days boiling up good hygiene. That's a two-week vacation spent boiling water each and every year. By the age of 10, we'd already invested more than 143 *days* slaughtering germs. When Cody turned 30, that would have tallied an entire *year* and two months. Before Cody came along, I was happy just reading dog-eared copies of *Reader's Digest* in the doc's reception room.

MeMe kuzamguma kiSwahili!

I can speak fluent Swahili, but the language of Cody's meds has always escaped me; it's not a 'romance language', making it hard for me to fathom.

I would sit in the admitting rooms or the doctor's offices worldwide for years, like I was deaf and dumb, as Bridget recounted the exact dosages, dates of Cody's last incarcerations, how many milligrams of this and that he was ingesting daily and more. Off the top of her head.

Because we shifted homesteads between the USA and Australia and other countries often, Bridget could convert from quarts and gallons to litres and milligrams without hesitation. For me it was in one partly deaf ear and out the daft one on the other side ... and gone. I was glowingly grateful for her complete dedication to all our kids on every front. Cody may have been dangling his legs over the hospital bed, but he was covertly tuned-in the entire time. Making mental notes.

What I didn't know then was that Bridget was also intentionally weening our son. She was making certain Cody was in attendance, and nothing was revealed or concealed in front of him to soften the situation. Bridget understood long before I did that if Cody were to make his way, one day he'd have to take on the CF fight and his illness solo. I was more inclined to avoid confrontations and provide pampering. Even covert cover-up. I had significant life experience at putting emotional band aids on everything. For me, the easiest way forward was to anchor my head in the sand when it came to unpleasantries. It worked fabulously fine for me in my youth. .

Movie mogul!

During one of Cody's incarcerations at the children's hospital, he had a chat with one of the volunteers for the Starlight Foundation and told her about his love of film and movies. She retold Cody's story and perhaps a month later, he was gifted with a fine camera and all the state-of-the-art equipment a young Steven Spielberg would need to make a movie. Cody made a few films and they're better than most amateur efforts. He made them with a good heart, even when he had trouble with his breathing on the 'set'. In high school he was asked to review movies for an outfit called Salty Popcorn which got him on the red carpet for heaps of film premieres. Cody stopped making films when he discovered girls. He hasn't used the camera in years, but he's still keenly interested in girls and movies. In that order.

Cody loved movies, and he put this passion to use getting himself a job at the Hoyt's theatre in the mall. He was 16 and he rocked up to the interview in a tracksuit, an hour late. His long-sleeved shirt covered the IV drip, so he could be reconnected when he returned to his hospital bed at Westmead. The interviewer never asked him if he had a life-threatening illness, or why he rocked up late, so he didn't feel compelled to enlighten her. Cody's gusto won the day and he got himself hired. Cody'd iron his uniform, shine his shoes and either Bridget or I would drop him off at work where he'd sweep up in-between flicks and dispense popcorn or sell tickets. He made some lifelong friends there. As his father, I was puffed up like a peacock and couldn't have been prouder. Cody was, for the most part, living the dream Bridget and I had wished for him: to be able to grow up as a normal kid. We'd intentionally avoided placing him on a 'disability list' or asking for financial assistance, and here was our son marching off to school and a job with a smile in his strut.

Cody did so well, he was rapidly promoted and this punk kid was made assistant manager. Our Cody was running a small empire, complete with an assistant manager's name tag. Cody worked alongside his pal Steve, a fella who would later go on to run other businesses and ask Cody to join him as part of his team. Ten years on, Steve asked Cody to be his best man and do the honors at his wedding. Good pals are very hard to come by.

Cody's moved on now, but he and I still 'do' about a new movie a week together, and we'll rent a classic, complete with his review of the flick afterwards. I love this, and always shout the popcorn and candy. I'm just happy to be invited. I almost never fall asleep in the movies anymore.

Tears here! I hate, love, hate the Facebook pages

I've seen firsthand the power of social media and Facebook to instantly alter my son's emotions. I love social media for its power to bring us closer to the ones we love and care for, and on the other side of the emotional fence, I hate the technology for the very same reasons. I've quietly stood by, Texas vigilant at Cody's bedroom door, when the news of yet another of his CF 'cystas' or 'fibros' dying is posted. Those kids could no longer hold on to the next breath.

I get out of bed in the middle of the night when I know one of Cody's pals is in trouble, and check to see what sunrise/sonrise will bring to his bedside. One morning, I learned that our son tearfully lost yet another of his 'cystas' in the USA, who could no longer hold out. She was three years younger than my boy. What our son does not know is I quietly send private messages to his buddies, or parents, or partners to remind them we have an 'entire army out here, hugging them'. In small measure, it helps me to get out of the sack.

Get out of his path ... that kid can dance!

At Cody's graduation from Glenaeon Montessori, students were invited to do a brief showcase, and I was surprised that our son stepped up and nominated to do a dance routine. He did a solo with fabulous style, and got the entire house standing when he was done. And then again, to my surprise, he invited any of his other, wonderful classmates to join him on stage, and my heart sank for him. For a moment, my pulse escalated, fearing what was coming: Cody, my wonderful son, standing alone on the stage without the support of his peers. I'd anticipated his humiliation when none of his classmates dared to take the stage. I was not upset for myself, but for my son, who honestly believed in the camaraderie of others and who was about to learn a valued lesson about not counting on the other guys to pull you through. The lesson learned was to be mine. Not only did two other classmates leap up from behind me, they were shouting encouragements to Cody – 'Hold on, I'm coming!' – as they peeled themselves down the aisles of folding chairs to get to the stage. They were wonderful and well synced, and the choreography couldn't have been finer, with my son, our Cody at the front of the group, leading by example.

I just want to be me! I'm moving out, even if it kills me!

When Cody's best buddy Jasper was at university, he located a townhouse to rent within walking distance of the campus, and asked Cody if he wanted to move in. Soulmates, flatmates, living the dream of young handsome blokes. Cody jumped at the notion, keen to attend his university classes like a local, visit the pub, sip good latte coffee, and eat the ample pies and pasta that were at hand just outside their terrace house's front door. The location was perfect, the place was not. Not even a blowtorch and dousing with DDT would eradicate the population of cockroaches, and even though we scoured the joint from top to bottom before moving Cody into his new abode, there still appeared to be a coating of 30-weight oil on everything. Cody loved, no, seized the notion that he could freewheel his life, and I'm not sure of it, but I think he played at the idea of living as if both his cystic fibrosis and diabetes did not exist at the time.

There were little clues about changes in his medical regime. For example, I was buying eight cases of nutrient supplements every few months, delivered to my place. And over the years, I knew that a palate of Ensure Plus had 24 boxes and little mini straws attached to the carton. When Cody was living at home, he'd knock off at least two a day. When I visited him and Jasper from time to time, I noted the wrappings were untouched, and nebulizers regularly used twice a day seemed to have a few days crust on them. He was having a good time, trying hard to keep up, but it was false bravado.

Some nosedives you cannot pull out of on your own

Trying to front up and just 'be himself' on campus was a downward spiral for Cody. I'm not sure how long Cody was away, but I was not surprised when he said he was keen to re-stake his claim on his bedroom at my place in Hollywood Lane. I was very excited to have him home but tried hard not be too overt in demonstrating my joy.

I'm a bit of a mother hen. For many weeks before our Dylan chose to move out I dangled shiny items in front of him to covertly try and convince him to stay: a new car, airline tickets and expensive band equipment if he'd stay home. Not even the offer of our three-car garage for his band practices prevailed. The new band house was in an area where nobody gave a turd if they played music all night, and I cringed quietly looking at the questionable neighborhood. I'm a bit of a location snob and pointed out the environs were far from anything resembling Beverly Hills. The pub on the corner boasted all-night naked girls, and three pawn shops seemed to be doing brisk business, even located next door to each other's establishments. On the day we moved Dylan into his new communal house in 'Deluge Hill', I spotted a sign for the real estate company that supports cystic fibrosis nationally called, LJ Hooker. When I proclaimed to the boys, 'Look there's a Hooker!' the boys were disappointed at my attempted humor.

They got that one wrong!

Cody-son turned 20 in 2009; in his first year, doctors said he would never live long enough to go to elementary school. They got that one wrong! Mind you, his quality of life is like a Coney Island roller-coaster. Cody is back on the 5th floor, growing some evil in his gunked-up lungs. I'm sleeping in the chair alongside his hospital bed; he opted for takeaway pizza, I went Chinese. We hosted the nurses' station with spring rolls and popcorn. His mom, here two nights in a row, has gone home to spend a bit of time under our own blanket, cuddling up with our other kids. Hayley spends more time in our bed now than she does in her own.

– Journal entry, November 2014

CHAPTER 16 | Make CF Stand for Cure Found!

For the first time ever, statistically, cystic fibrosis sufferers over the age of eighteen now outnumber those who can't hold on and don't make it. This stat is a real line in the sand, signaling a true change in the future for all of us who have come to the battlefield to fight CF. Although the current margin is measured in tiny, short hairs, it does signal a positive change in the outlook. We mourn for the kids who could not hold out and continue to breathe through a straw any longer. Tears here.

We live in wonderful times ... if you've got a few million dollars to spare

When people ask me what kind of boat I'm on now, I pull the photo of our three kids out of my wallet. The one with the kids waving little flags at the curb-side on the 4th of July 1999 and say: It's 110 feet long and has a heliport on the rear deck. Right alongside the jacuzzi. It's insured by Lloyds and her tax-free home port is ... my imagination.

– Journal entry

According to Google, The cost for Pulmozyme inhalation solution (2.5 mg/2.5 ml) is around $3608 for a supply of 75 millilitres, depending on the pharmacy you visit in the USA. You'll need to order this much, say, four to five times a year. Budget for $18,000–20,000 depending on state and local taxes. You'll need to then add a few hours each month for the paperwork required, and an additional $4000 a month for your medical coverage provider. There's a fair bit more you'll need from the folks at the pharmacy; you'll get to know them on a first-name basis. I've made a habit of dropping in with a fresh fruit basket or chocolates when I collect medications and prescriptions. I've vowed to never go empty-handed, or neglect to say thank you for taking an interest in my loved ones.

I've said from the very beginning that Cody would not be with us today if a whole heap of other dynamic things, discoveries and dedicated folks hadn't stayed the course. Not everyone can access these drugs and breakthroughs have a cost, quite literally. Kalydeco, Vertex's original CF breakthrough, has a list price of $311,000 per patient per year. Orkambi, a less-effective drug combination that works for more patients than Kalydeco, is priced at $272,000 annually. I think it took constant hammering in Canberra to secure the approval of this drug and I can't bear to count the number of Cody's CF 'cystas' and 'fibros' who could no longer hold out.

Sir Richard's Virgins

In 2009, with the help of Sir Richard Branson, we painted up my 1960s VW Kombi to look like one of Richard's planes, complete with the Vargas-like 1930s Virgin girls on the body. Our CF 'flair-craft' boasted portholes and tiny tail feathers, turning heads everywhere. Richard bellied-up for matching funds to mine, and we entered the cystic fibrosis Great Escape Oz Car Rally in outback Australia. Ten days of eating dust, time checkpoints, pub lunches, fabulous stargazing and great company along the way. Cattle and sheep stations along the route played host, and in towns Rotary Clubs cooked up meals for about 150 of us. Of the 58 cars that started, 41 finished. Our trusted and rusted old, air-cooled ride was awarded the humorously coveted, 'We Never Thought You'd Make the Finish Line' award!'

Each team entry was encouraged to raise donation dollars and create a theme. Prizes were to be awarded for both costuming and colorful embellishments to the cars. Cody's crew went along merrily as Sir Richard's 'virgins' (oddly, nobody believed us!), while other teams adapted the uniforms and costumes of superheroes, reprobates and angels. Other entries also came creatively dressed as the Hulk, and circus clowns. One foursome came along in goatees and green canvas cover-all's, with a car painted up to resemble a moving outhouse to 'make a deposit' like the legendary Australian mockumentary of the portaloo, *Kenny*.

On the advice of his entire medical team, Cody was told he had to give the rally a miss. And they were right on the money; over 10 days I sucked up all manner of outback red dust, bull dust and grit. Blowing my nose turned my hanky orange-red and my toothbrush had a baby-powder coating of outback grit on it. Even with the windows closed we accumulated inch-deep dunes of very fine, silt-like dust in the cockpit of our Kombi.

I'm going! Even if it kills me!

Along on that dust-covered trek was a clean-shaven and chiseled good-looking young fella named Peter. I never did get Peter's last name, but he'd been kicked about a fair bit by his CF. He'd signed on and entered the fun- and fundraiser despite repeated medical advice and numerous loved-one-warnings of the brutally unforgiving and rough outback conditions. The likelihood of sucking in huge bits of Australian rust-red dust and melting/sweltering heat along the track were the only bits of news he would be getting. Organizers made Peter sign significant release-from-liability waivers. Three of them.

Peter was determined. He would go along even if his medical team and anyone (make that everyone) else told him not to. 'I told the doc, I'm going! Even if it kills me! My doctor said in reply that the odds were highly likely it would do just that,' Peter told me over the campfire and a pint of lager on a cattle station the size of the state of Rhode Island.

He adamantly refused to put his life on hold, a notion Cody cloned without ever having met the fella. 'Pedro', as I renamed him after several stout beers, was 28. He'd already defied the scientific odds, having lived a good 20 years beyond his statistical expiration date. Peter gave me hope. I saw my son in him, one day, heading towards 30. And years later, when Cody-son and I visited hospital bedsides in the USA, I could understand why parents and grandparents of CF kids cried openly when Cody entered the room. Cody delivered *hope* alongside those tiny Captain America teddy bears.

Pedro, alongside his furry-bearded MASH co-driver played their parts as medical nurses to a T. They shaved their narrow legs, wore white support stockings (at night in the pub, sporting garters for the troops) and seductively cross-dressed daily as female caregivers. The toilet-bowl brothers, The 'Kennys', suggested the duo, decked out in those skimpy white skirts would go down well in the mostly-male Opal mining town of Coober Pedy. After a few pints in a middle-of-outback Australia pub, Pedro planted an apple-red kiss on me. I left the lipstick there as a badge of honor. People took photos!

Their outfits seemed well-suited to their 'ride': a beat-to-hell-and-back 1960s ambulance, a massive red cross, hand-painted brazenly along its girth. The uniforms melded to make a medically perfect wardrobe match for the dynamic duo. Only on day five, did I learn Pedro's furry-faced co-driver could neither speak nor hear. Someone forgot to tell this dynamic duo they were physically challenged or impaired. Pedro was a siren of hope to everyone who went along.

Peter, Peter, red-dust eater!

Peter slept nightly next to our Kombi on an ambulance stretcher under the night-time stars of Australia's Southern Cross. Alongside his swag, he bedded down a white oxygen tank that fed his facemask, an all-too-familiar puke-green 'puffer', and an inhaler. Under the pillow he kept his insulin, and blood sugar testing kit. I estimated he was downing about 30 pancreatic enzyme tablets a day on tour. I didn't ask.

Peter happily kept a roll of crisp, new $50 bills tucked into his padded brassiere during the daytime rally drives. He was ready and willing to pay 'fines' each day when our rally encountered premeditated, hilariously daft fundraising roadblocks.

> *Today I was stopped on a lone red track by a trio of flack-jacketed and armed, authentic New South Wales police officers. They unjustly lobbed my Adonis-like body into handcuffs. Other rally participants cheered as my modest, well-mannered and moderately-innocent arse, encased in irons like Ned Kelly, was summarily and mercilessly tossed into the back of a caged jail wagon for the high offenses of speaking with a funny American accent and having nicked what was clearly, Sir Richard Branson's ride! It was all fabulous fun and folks filmed my farewell in-car incarceration speech.*
>
> *– Journal entry, August 2009*

I paid numerous 'fines' with great glee as donations were creatively collected daily and went into another big bucket for finding a CF cure. Other on-rally offenses imposed on members of our rally gang included legal offenses such as 'cross-dressing while crossing a cattle crossing', 'being bloody wankers' or in my case, 'talk'n' like a septic-tank Yank'! I bad.

I had a great time, met some fabulous folks and I'd happily go again one day. Provided I could do it in my pal Kamahl's ocean-blue Rolls Royce. With the windows up, AC on full, seated in the back, keeping company with the open bar ...

Back on track

The most inspiring thing about this remarkable young man was Peter's perpetual smile, his willingness to chip in and help, and his ocean-deep sense of humor that would have put Jay Leno or Johnny Carson on their butts. When on day one Peter was given the task of emptying the big after-breakfast rubbish bins with me, he cheered and did a little circle dance like a lottery winner. I followed his lead and danced my best jig alongside him. It was one of the best assignments I've had. Ever!

Peter was fully committed to living to the top of his ability. He took the extra puffers he had to manage over nightly campfires, swallowed perhaps 1000 pancreatic enzymes in the course of the 10-day rally, and injected himself with insulin. The fella was a purebred walking advertisement for staying on the tracks, while toting along a smile laced with *hope*.

Peter could sometimes be seen (usually as his rickety ambulance overtook my pathetically sluggish VW Kombi) wearing a previously white, dust-covered surgical mask. We all knew he was smiling underneath it.

Knowing I disdain body art of any kind, Cody had a tattoo embedded in his shoulder when I was away years later: cut into him, in calligraphy and Latin it says 'seize the day!'

Peter, our Cody, and the thousands of other CFers I've met, have learned the delight and the pure joy of just being here, the ability to contaminate others with smile and that 'just breathing' is a blessing. Even If you need to inhale life through a straw. Before Cody, I took this totally for granted. I believed I was bulletproof.

Hoping for further breakthroughs

Collectively, we raised over $500,000 and had one hell of a good time doing it. At night, in my swag under the stars of the Southern Cross, I wished we had Cody along for the ride to share this experience; then I'd stop myself, recalling earlier when blowing my nose, the handkerchief in my palm went copper-colored for all the bull dust we'd been breathing. The road rally traversed some of Australia's most remote, and dust-red landscape, with breakdowns hourly. For Cody, and other CFers, we'd simply capture as many photos as possible to share from way out there!

As if on cue in 1989, for the birth of our Cody, a pair of scientists discovered and isolated the mutant gene responsible for cystic fibrosis. From then on, this breakthrough would lead to almost monthly updates and clinical suggestions and improvements on how to better manage and treat an illness without a cure. The research and funding floodgates opened wide, and even as I write, great strides are being made daily, the pace quickens, and CF families see a smoother stretch of the road ahead of them. Pharmaceutical companies, seeing huge upsides in creating profits for improvements, lead the pack. We're just happy they are keen!

CHAPTER 17

Our Cody Is Still Standing, and Still Fighting Because of His Mother

We never really discussed it, but Bridget and I made a pact: a promise to each other over our rickety, homemade, scrap wood table to do anything we could to keep Cody. Anything. The table has always wobbled on unsteady legs, but our resolve to bring up our son as close to happy, and as normal as possible never faltered. Not once.

Twenty years later, in a different kitchen, in a different country, on a different continent, and across the same makeshift table, Bridget and I would agree to dissolve our pact as life partners.

Bridget had every right to want to step away from me, and I should have been stronger, and fought harder to hold onto her.

But we agreed with one tearful voice, to fight side-by-side, and give whatever it took, for our three wonderful offspring. Our children are the strongest glue that binds us together, and we'd vowed to never use them as a jackhammer or a wedge.

Because we did so much travel in the early years, my melding to my mother was special. When I got older, I used to think about the possibility of losing one or the other, and in every case, I had to admit to the fact that I'd much prefer to lose my dad, than my mom. I think most kids play this same game out in their heads at some time. When I mentioned this to my dad, he said most sons would agree with him; he said he felt the same way as a boy.

– Cody

Burning Bridget at the stake

More than a decade ago, I threw out of my life the most important person in it. I drove Bridget away with a venom in my fangs, releasing words and emotions that should not be cast, even on the worst of enemies. I doused her internally with emotional mustard gas that singed her heart. Bridget did not just need to leave; for her it was a matter of survival. And although there may not be a jury anywhere who could convict me of it, I emotionally, if not literally, tortured the one person who gave me everything worthwhile in my adult life. I will spend the rest of my life trying to cauterize, in part, those wounds.

The missing wedding ring

I hunted for days through the house, looking for my wedding ring without luck. I'd quietly asked each of the kids and the weekly housekeeper if they'd come across it. I never took it off, not once in years.

I have always, worn my wedding ring with great pride of ownership; I belonged to someone, with someone, for the rest of my life. It gave me a great, silent sense of belonging. I waved it about with great pride, saying in later years yep, I was 'married three times' ... pausing for the shock-effect to sink in, and then closing with 'all of them to the very same, wonderful woman'.

One morning, about a month before we split, I asked Bridget why she'd stopped wearing her wedding ring. She'd been away a lot of late, we hardly talked, hugged or cuddled. She was doing courses to establish her Kahuna massage business, investing in her independence. Quietly, I thought this was a good idea with all of my brood; especially as my entire plan for leaving a solid financial footing for them when I died was shattered. Bridget's answer was easy; she had to take the ring off when massaging customers, and she sometimes forgot to put it back on. I read the message differently and her ring never again materialized.

When Bridget and I started coming apart, it was fully my doing. I hold a grudge, and the closer I am to the issue, the tighter I squeeze. Anything was possible with her in my life. Bridget was my religion. To this day, we've never spoken of it, but I stopped praying, and started retaliation in the only form I knew. I withdrew from my life partner, from grab-assing, and jumping on our bed. I welcomed the notion that Hayley could lodge herself between us, and I'd escape to the guest bedroom for my 'snoring'. And I waited for Bridget to save me; she promised she would fight tooth and nail, she would. It took a solid, ugly six months of skirting around each other for her to confront me, saying that she needed to get out, take her own space, and go. She was convinced I was having an affair (I was contemplating this, but not out of passion, out of spite) and I left my wife no option but to save herself. I'd driven off, and out, the most important person in my entire life through my bitterness and hatred. I was torn apart, at a time when I should have been reaching out to my wife, who was in my mind, already making plans without me.

> *I've been waking up at Hollywood Lane at 2 or 3 am, it's like the outer casing of me is OK to the eye, but the innards are missing. Like some machinery has vacuumed my emotions out of me, and I'm scared I'll live the rest of my life like this. I've inherited my mother's emotional Achilles high heels, and there is no route back to the way things were. I've thrown out of my life with true hatred the only person I've ever truly loved to the core and done it with such a venom injection. Leaving no room for reconciliation. I'm capable of inflicting extreme pain. It is so painful, that I repeatedly mask it in excuses and accolades and testimonials.*
>
> *I no longer sleep in our marital bed; our daughter has filled that void as I've populated the guest bedroom for months on end now … I used to love the notion of her, my princess crawling between Bridget and me. Now, she appears as a roadblock to my ever reclaiming*

*forgiveness from my wife. Texas dawg has become my
new bed fellow.*

— **Journal entry, Peppercorn Drive, Sydney**

Life unravels rapidly

Make no bones about it. When you are gifted with kids,
especially special needs ones, it puts massive pressures
on a relationship. Before our son was born, Bridget and
I happily flitted about with options, made plans at what
seemed like the drop of a hat, and altered our lives over an
evening dinner out. Lazy Sunday afternoons on the beach
at Sullivan's Island, outside of Charleston, eating early-batch
chocolate croissants from the local baker's oven and reading
the papers, our big choice was which place we'd test on the
way home for eats.

The stress of having a first-born son with cystic fibrosis
was buried, and I followed the lead of Bridget, who was
simply determined to press ahead with this new gift we'd
been given. On the surface I was laminated emotionally,
internally I felt like I was afflicted with rinderpest, that inner-
ear maggot that burrows in the brain of African animals and
festers until the animal simply walks in circles, churning the
grassland into dust until it can stand no longer.

I'd always jokingly said that Bridget was my religion, but
I never meant it more honestly than when she took the lead
and pressed ahead with Cody's health. I was sure then my
wife would go the distance, whatever distance that would
become, to make sure our son would win.

When I'm under pressure, I digress and find comfort in
the things that are easy for me to accomplish. Small, baby

steps in arenas that feel comfortable to me, and when confronted with the medical facts of Cody's CF, I fled the room emotionally. I couldn't seem to grasp the details of pancreatic enzymes, daily airway clearance, or nebulized and exactly measured bowls of medicines. But I could fathom and come to the table with the concept that what Cody really needed was money. Lots and lots of money. This was a sandbox I could fathom. Taking the path of least agony for me, I elected to leave Cody's care in the fabulous hands of my wife, while I was able to leave the house, carry on my way, and the only significant difference was the upped ante needed to make ends meet. For years I'd do this, flipping between campaigns and projects, consulting work and out-of-town assignments, all the while knowing, that Cody was being fully tended at home, a dedication to our son, stronger than any super glue ever engineered.

I don't believe, in over 21 years, my wife ever really took a day off from looking after our children.

When Bridget finally said she was leaving, she'd already left

My wife had no choice: I'd already told her words no person should ever be allowed to share with another. I played with, and practiced those words for days, even weeks beforehand to be sure they cut sharper than any Sabatier knife. Bridget had no choice but to run from Peppercorn Ridge for her sanity. I'd emotionally tortured her, excommunicated her for months in the lead up to her going. Our children watched it fester, caustic to the touch. It was Dylan who first asked me what the hell was going on, followed within days by his older brother.

I'd ruined the most important person in my life.

Years later, this time when I was certain my death was right over the next ridge, I penned a note in a bottle and tossed it into Narrabeen Reserve. It got caught up in the marsh reeds, and afraid someone might actually find it, I tried wading into the shallows to secure its return. The pluff mud under my feet was so very foul, I retreated to the shoreline. The stench reminded me of that childhood dare, which nearly got me killed.

> *I'm an unforgivable ass. I know that now, but I am going to try, and keep on trying to tell you what having you in my life has meant.*
>
> *I've never said it, and only now, am I beginning to understand that you have been my religion; I foolishly blindly, even callously, stopped praying for a time. An act of cowardice and ego on my part, for which there is no sufficient confession, no penance, no performance, perfume, or trinket of jewelry sufficient enough to mend the wounds I've made inside of you.*
>
> *But please, with the same strength you possess, that has carried us this far together, reach into your heart and give me the smallest bit of hope we can one day again enjoy the sheer joy we had in our very first days as husband and wife. I'm emotionally breathing through a wooden straw only now, taking half breaths.*
>
> *Please, I need you to help me breathe fully again.*
>
> **– Undelivered message in a bottle**

You can't do this alone!

Any family with a loved one toting a chronic illness will readily tell you that the hoops, the frustrations and the paperwork involved in the system is debilitating, dehumanizing, and dynamic in nature. It is a never-ending story. In defense of the system in place to help, barriers have been set up to prevent folks from defrauding the system, and there is no question this takes place. Years ago, I met a fellow who seemed ever-present and parasitic. If someone at the other end on the bar gave the 'round for the bar' he'd double up and move his choice from 'well drink' to top-shelf grog. The bastard rarely tipped. When I asked him how he came to have time and money, he claimed to be a tailor by trade. It was a great job, better than winning at the track, his other venue of choice. One day, he got a tiny needle from the sewing machine through his finger and applied for lifetime disability. He proudly shared the story of how he marched into Social Security, went through the paperwork, and applied for complete disability. They even gave him a sticker to hang over the car mirror. This chap said he'd been paid sweetly for the past seven years and counting and lived rent free with his mother. He'd just ordered a new Lincoln to take him to the track.

There is a CF Avengers gal whom my son loves in the USA. He sends her money he does not have for her medicines because she's given up doing the same paperwork, and standing in the same lines, under fluorescent bulbs. If the shitheads are going to fly under the radar anyway, let's loosen up, get the goods and services to the folks who need them and pay a handsome bounty to anyone who can dob in a blood-sucking bastard!

When Cody did finally genuflect and reach out for public assistance, the paperwork was daunting. At one stage, I guessed at least a dozen pulp trees had been felled to document Cody's condition, and he'd already sent across reams of the paperwork, and perhaps 100 pounds of medical professionals' documents, each with phone numbers for verification. Just in case Cody was trying to pull the medical wool over anyone's eyes. And yet, the system insisted on sighting our son. As an alternative, I suggested they send someone to the ICU ward during visiting hours: one of his family members would happily step aside for the 30-second interview. They might want to rent a van to take a fraction of the corroborating paperwork back to the office with them when they went.

I was placed on hold for some time, then advised by a supervisor's voice that I had not filled out the proper forms to act or speak on my son's behalf. Road rage might be renamed on my police file as 'Code rage!' When I'd hung up Bridget reminded me that the agency on the other end of the phone 'recorded all calls for training and verification purposes' and I should expect a visit from the authorities. Maybe even the terrorism fellas might phone.

The icing on the bureaucratic cake came when I took a call on Cody's phone while he was in the intensive care unit and a voice at Centrelink formally advised that if Cody elected to cancel his medical evaluation interview, he'd have to wait at least, another seven weeks to reschedule. It had taken our son over four months to get this one. I felt obligated to bite my tongue on my son's behalf, while pointing out the facts to the mercurial voice on the other end of the line: the scheduled 'evaluation' meeting required Cody to drive an hour each way, wait in a crowded reception area, where he'd be exposed to all manner of the common cold and other ailments, only to finally stand in front of Centrelink's appointed doctor, to confirm the fact that for his entire life he had cystic fibrosis and for 15 years, diabetes?!

Hayley asked us all, gathered around the Sunday evening dinner table how she too could qualify for a concession card for whopping huge discounts. Before Cody could pass a comment across the table, Bridget said, 'All Cody had to do was be born with a chronic Illness, that could very well kill him.'

> *I went to collect a cold beer from the bowels of the refrigerator this afternoon, and on the door, in Cody's own finely done hand, was written his own take on Nietzsche: 'Whatever does not kill me had f^*king better start running!'*
>
> *I don't know what had inspired it, Cody rarely needs to use foul verbiage, but I knew what he was saying.*
>
> *– Journal entry, 2016*

CHAPTER 18

Reluctant Changes

> 'Smile because you woke up
> this morning and you can.
> Smile because you own the air
> in your lungs, the blood in your
> veins and the love in your heart.
> Smile.'
>
> – Facebook comment from
> Andie Jessup, one of Cody's CF
> Avengers (RIP)

Burning the birthday candle at both ends

On Cody's 24th birthday I purchased a fire-engine red T-shirt at a cystic fibrosis fundraiser which read: 'Someone I LOVE needs a CURE!' I don't normally wear T-shirts but I'm proud to put this one on, even if it's a bit too small for me around my ever-expanding midriff.

Cody spent a great deal of time planning his 25th birthday celebrations, sending invites, laying down the musical score, theming the event around the Great Gatsby and getting our backyard party ready. But he was attempting to run under the radar. He was silently very sick, and overtly determined to make it happen until we airlifted him into a hospital bed two days before the event, and he was forced to call the whole thing off. His health was rotten but his emotional weather was in the toilet.

We did our best to decorate his hospital room with birthday banners, his bevy of lovely nurses baked cookies at home, and his room was a constant revolving door of visitors who came at all hours. Medical staff who knew and loved Cody turned a blind eye or two to the formal visitors' hours posted everywhere, and we had a candle-less cake which played 'Happy Birthday' over and over until the battery gave up. He came out three weeks later with his lungs working much better. It wasn't the backyard bash he'd been planning, but we were all happy he'd made it this far. For Cody, reaching the age of 25 was a significant milestone, even if he had to spend it in the hospital. Many of Cody's younger 'cystas' and 'fibros' sadly didn't get this far.

Flying high, only this time with oxygen on board

It's a dark and chilly morning at 5 am, and I'm grinding my teeth almost non-stop as Cody prepares to head off to the USA in under a week's time. I shiver when he reminds me, that he's 'determined to do this, even if it's the last thing I ever do!', Which is a throw-away cliché normally, but in Cody's case it could very well be fact.

He's pulling himself off the bed 'no matter what!' and going to the city for a meeting of CF professionals. I think it's our fifth medical meeting this month, and today is only the twelfth.

Cody hit the bedsheets early with a pain in his spleen. Only a week earlier the location of his spleen caused Bridget and I to laugh uncontrollably, as we sat in the transplant specialist's office. Cody was shirtless, on the examining table for a once-over during the consultation. The doc, who had done these exams countless times before, made an off-the-cuff comment on feeling Cody's liver, and Cody calmly corrected him, saying, 'But Doc, you do realize, that's my *spleen*, right?!'

I'd looked over in disbelief at Bridget, who was shivering quietly with laughter, trying hard to conceal herself. When she looked at me, we both burst – I was in tears, Bridget handing me tissues from her handbag to wipe the pent-up deluge. The doc and Cody both looked at us laughing uncontrollably, as if to say 'What the fu**k!?' and when we could breathe again, I made a feeble attempt to explain the humor and the emotional release of pent-up tension. Both the doctor and Cody got the joke.

Cody had just matter-of-factly corrected the specialist doctor on the location of his body parts.

'Cystas and fibros, start your nebulizers!'

Cody was determined to rub elbows and other CF body parts with other CFers, who gather once a year to cover a 5-kilometre (3 mile) stretch of Daytona Beach Florida. They mingle freely, despite warnings from medicos worldwide about the potential for cross-infection to just 'breathe the same salty air'.

Cody has his own pit crew: a dedicated team of his parents, siblings, his CF team, and a ton of tremendous pals who pull out all the stops, to ensure he gets to go along. Cody declared his intention to our family almost before he stepped off the plane: he *was* going to be going back to Daytona with the other CFers next time around.

Texas dawg under Cody's bed. This is bad, really bad

There was no laughter in Cody's dark room. Texas knew things were not good, taking up his protector's post under Cody's bed and staying there – only his moist, stubby black nose poked out, and he would ignore all my bribe offers of biscuits to extract him from his station. X-rays of our son had revealed that his spleen was three times the size of mine, or anyone else's. As his liver failed, Cody's spleen had to go into overdrive. Not a good gear to be in, it caused him great pain, which he did his best to mask publicly. I made up hot water bottles, which temporarily eased the pain, and bring him his meds in bed. All these activities only bandaids and cosmetic blankets to mask his real situation.

Cody had been looking forward to a sit-down with a pricey psychologist to let loose his story and spill the sputum/beans about his spleen and other failing body parts. He came home depressed, saying for $300 (he totes my credit card in his wallet for all things medical related) he got nothing. Zero. Zilch. Nada.

The expected connection just wasn't there, and ugly fluorescent overhead lighting hadn't helped set the stage for sharing. I said he should just try again, until, like other paths we'd traveled, he found the right one. Keep the credit card in your wallet son, use it whenever you need to. That's why it has your name on it.

Sharing sour pipes

In our childhood home, my mother penned a note that we hung on the guestroom bathtub. It said: 'Our home is old, The pipes are sour, You can take a bath but PLEASE no shower'! One of our house guests was blind, and the entire kitchen ceiling below that bathroom required redoing after his visit.

Our cottage on Hollywood Lane is a bit like that; it's an old fibro house (fibro being the operative cover-up for 'asbestos clad') we happily call home. The asbestos is fine, we just make sure we don't crack into any of it. But the walls are wafer thin and you can feel every footfall on the random plank timbers. When Hayley stays, she says she can hear my snoring, two rooms off. I suggest she's prone to exaggerations, but the kid's right. Oddly, we're Americans living in Newport Beach, on Hollywood Lane in Australia.

I hear Cody's nightly coughing and can tell better than a hand-delivered telegraph when it's exceptionally lousy breathing for him. I've heard it said that people who live near the traintracks for a time, become immune to passing traffic. They no longer hear the trains. I hear every single Cody cough.

I'm up at 5 am: it's winter, cold and dark, and Texas dog has repeatedly refused to leave his den at the foot of Cody's bed to make his morning turds. I'm forced to lure him out, and only get him to move by offering up a 'brisket'. A 'brisket' is a cross-dressed bribe melded into a biscuit. The cat, Scratch, comes willingly, staggering behind us in the middle of Hollywood Lane like a drunken sailor. Whenever the rare car appears, she flies for home, running sideways as if her backside is trying to out-distance her front end. I never knew cats ran like this; all the lions, and leopards and cheetahs I've seen pierce the track like an arrow. I'm halfway down the laneway, and I can still, hear Cody coughing. I can already envision the see-through plastic cup, half sputum, half a deep maroon-red blood spoor lining the cup. Cody camouflages this concoction sometimes when it's bad, loading up the cup with Kleenex to avoid me prodding him about the contents. If I could, I'd keep him in bed today.

This is another bad one, and despite this, Cody will be trying very hard to get to his office today. I'll try to lure him into the notion of taking the day off to rest, but I know my suggestion is going to fall onto muted ears. When Cody makes up his mind, for better or worse, I reluctantly stand aside. Cody says 'good people are counting on him'.

My often-angry reply is, 'You're no fucking good to anyone if you peg!'

Today Cody is insisting on getting to his office, even if it means hobbling along on one leg, for an all-in staff meeting and then a celebratory CF Foundation lunch. People are counting on him to do his report. Sometimes I accuse him of thinking he is bulletproof; sometimes he admits to being a bit more wounded. I'll drive him to the city, he can load up his nebulizer and regroup his energies on the commute, and to most outside observers, they'll not have a clue he's drawing on every vapor of strength he can muster to just 'be present'.

I remind our son I've got nothing to do today and can happily pick him up for the homeward commute. He knows I'm lying, but smiles, saying he'll try and give me an hour's notice. He doesn't need to, I'll hover.

Someone great once said, 'Anxiety is nothing short of death by a thousand small wounds'.

– Journal entry

Workplace pleasures!

Cody absolutely loves his job with Palliative Care Australia, which keeps him fully engaged three days a week. It also allows him time for his cystic fibrosis and diabetes clinics, home visits for physiotherapy and to on rare occasions a chance to recharge his batteries and sleep in until the crack of noon. The people in his office love him right back. He is inspirational, and we admire the way he will muster, and get himself out of bed in the dark 'because people are counting on him'. His words, not his father's – there are many days I want to point him back into his bed, surround him with his dog and cat, and remind him he needs to rest.

Cody is the very best board member we've ever had

> CF means having to swallow 40 tables a day to digest your food.
> CF means two hours of treatment every day to clear your lungs.
> CF means a very short life.
> THERE Is NO CURE.

The freestanding banner stands like a sentinel at the front door of the CF Foundation annual general meeting. It's the same one they erect at the starting line for the cystic fibrosis Great Strides walks and other special events. The image depicts a pretty, healthy-looking young CF patient, holding forward a huge banquet platter of multicolored pills and nebulizer medicines, masks, tubes and vials the CF lass *needs* to just breathe every day. The letters are fat so you can read it in passing, and I wish it were all a lie.

Cody reminds me, on the way to the meeting, he lives for 'CF' – cure found!

Cody sees straight through my camouflaged request to attend his meeting. For my sake mostly, 'the captain' plays along, offering alternative suggestions for how I might otherwise better spend my day. I discount them all. Cody's included that I'd much rather spend my Sunday morning walking the dog and collecting small Texas turds in plastic bags, annoying the neighbors with an early morning lawn mower, or gliding his mom's old, flamingo-pink bike without brakes onto our beachfront. Actually, Cody doesn't know that the front tire's been flat for weeks.

'Sorry my son, all those suggested options are way too boring! Why do that when I can drive you crazy as my captive audience! You'll helplessly have to listen to my weekly vents and issues, and a few of my more spectacularly savory missives about global warming, world poverty, lousy drivers, crap on TV, and my disdain for tattoos!'

We both know the real agenda behind me wanting to tag along. Cody is also an exceptional driver, which compels him to remind me sometimes of his skills. He's been known to apply my indicators for me. He and my daughter, the Princess Hayley are, massive and articulate back-seat drivers. I don't think Dylan would care one wink if he never had to drive again any eon soon. When Dylan's in cars, he might as well be on Mars.

If I drive, Cody can conserve his limited energy and I'll be able to deposit him close to the front door. He'll stride into the board room meeting like he's fit for a 65 Roses Walkathon and shake hands like a farmer's one-armed water pump. I can park the car miles away and race back to listen in from the back of the room as a late comer. Cody leads: I try to remain invisible.

For the journey, Cody packs a cooler bag full of meds that require refrigeration and a tote full of other must-have items. We look like we're headed for an extended outback camel safari. During the round trip Cody will load up and shallowly inhale his nebulizer meds, using an expensive little air pump (it cost five times more than my very first car!) which he runs off the car's cigarette lighter. He'll fill red plastic cups with some very vile mucus plugs drawn from deep down in his lungs. We've stopped getting the see-through ones because he knows it upsets me to see his blood, and green-yellow plugs fill the cups every day. I've lied to him before, getting the clear cups and saying the shop was sold out of the others.

Cody is already exhausted, but I know from experience, he'll give the meeting absolutely everything, smile broadly as he discreetly coughs bloody drool into Kleenex tissues that he cleverly buries in his jacket pocket. Cody's handsome, and has some nice color in his shallow cheeks, having spent an hour in the sun the day before. Cody looks like a slender poster-kid for CFers 'doing remarkably, fabulously, well'. Even though he's rotting away totally on his insides. I'm keen to scream, 'Fuck off everyone, can't you *see* or *hear*? He's faking it!'

A young mother, with a CF two-year-old son, approaches me afterwards to say how very inspirational it is to see Cody, in his twenties doing so well: 'He's so full of life and energy and seems so very fit!' She's doing what I do, grabbing onto images of her child doing fine in the future. My son can often change color like a chameleon, depending on what leaf he needs to be nesting on. I don't have the heart, or the right to enlighten this new mother with my crystal ball. I won't tell her my son is lying. She'll make these heart-destroying discoveries in her own time. Cody would be deeply disappointed with me if I honestly told her the real story of how my son is rapidly approaching the end of the line.

Sharing the cottage on Hollywood Lane means ...

Sharing the same bathroom, and I've made discoveries about my champion Cody that never really revealed themselves fully when we were in a sprawling home with five bathrooms to play about in. My first discovery, call it a toiletry enlightenment even, was that my son refuses to change the cardboard core of a toilet paper roll! When I first made the connection with seeing the brown core on the wall-side dispenser, I approached my handsome son to suggest that if he used up the last of the butt-crack wipes, he was morally obligated to replace the roll from one of the zillion new rolls we keep by the bale-full, like hay on hand – I buy toilet paper by the bulk load.

To this day, don't know how Cody calculates it down to the last butt-soft square, left there like a cattle rustler hanging from a tree, for me. It's just one small loop of TP, hardly enough for any sized butt at all.

Cody promised to oblige, but I could already see the grinders working through his Cheshire grin – he'd simply avoid having to change the paper roll by assuring he never exposed himself to the last square. I give him huge credos for his solution; even if it means reaching for my piece of tissue only to discover the white, last square, dangling there! When openly confronted about it, we both laugh at the insignificance of it all. That's just how we roll around here. Cody is a household disaster about picking up around the cottage but I remind myself he's the best housemate I could ever ask for. We laugh on occasion when I point out that all his laundry seems content to surround the empty laundry hamper. Or I point to the sink and give my son a brief historical background for what it's meant to be used for. When I jokingly asked Cody what he thought those two convenient handles on the side of the garbage bin might be for, his faster-than-a-speeding-bullet reply bent me over in stitches of laughter. 'Dad! Don't you know those are there to make YOUR life easier!'

– Journal entry, 2016

I AM, my father's son

Only when I, like my old man, started being away from home, did I begin to understand my father's joy in doing the dishes with his kids helping. He was giving our mother some time to herself, which she'd often use to stay at the kitchen table flipping the pages of a magazine while we cleared, washed, rinsed and dried. My father was connecting himself to his family, while making an event and a stage for us to share. He'd grill us on school days, and how one of us came to be wearing a cast, or suggest a place where we might go 'digga-digga' in the family station wagon on Sunday. It was years later that I understood that for my dad, and myself, the going away we did for our work was never really an adventure. It was more like a mandatory self-exile. You fly to put food on the table.

Driving Cody in the dark

Last night Cody had some serious blood spoor in his sputum cup, and I jumped at the chance to have him reconsider going to catch his two-hour-long bus ride to his office at 6 am. He was determined to go ahead, there were people counting on him there. When Cody is committed, it takes more than a mandate from his mom and dad, or even his CF team speaking with one voice, to make him change his path.

If he wants to get to the office by 8, the guys needs to wake up at 4.30 am to knock off all the meds, and nebs, and 'stuff' he has to do to just get out of the front door. So I offered an alternative: he could sleep in the extra hour, and I'd drive him to the city, and drop him on the office front doorstep. And during the commute, he could do his two nebulizers, a flutter to clear his airways, discreetly fill a plastic cup with ugly sputum, and even listen to a wonderful monologue from his 'old man'.

I've been doing this shuttle for a little over a year now, not every day, just twice weekly, and we've gotten so good at it, the entire round trip for me takes under three hours. And I'm stopping for a leak and a cup of coffee in the middle. I think Cody enjoys the ride as much as I do. The morning front lawn has a mild dandruff cover of white, and the grass crunches like candy-apple glazing under my feet. I'm wearing flip-flops, which are clearly the wrong gear. There is a thin coat of frost on the windshield of my son's car.

– Journal entry

Tomorrow Cody has to be out west at the hospital by 7 am for more tests and probes. They'll knock him about gently, and he'll be 'put under' so he'll need a designated driver. When there's a coin toss for who takes him on these occasions, I think he prefers to have his mom along. Bridget is steady and level-headed: his old man leapfrogs emotionally and is noted for overreacting and a fair bit of knee-jerking. His mom is happy to sit by his recliner in the recovery room, silent, and just read her book. Cody says she never asks to share any of his jelly.

Turning 26

Cody attacked his plan for his 26th birthday bash with a 'dam the torpedoes, full steam ahead' attitude. His Facebook invite list lit up like the decorations on a Christmas tree, a massive white marquee filled the backyard, and we upgraded the chrome barbecue to accommodate feeding a few hundred revelers. Robbed of his quarter-century event, Cody was going full hog and I was the cook.

I knew in advance he was headed for the wrecking ball with his health, but he took me aside to say he was just trying to live as best he could, and if it meant his 26th was to be his last, he was going out in style. I pledged whatever support I could give, and my lips were to remain sealed as he faked being well enough to the other loved ones around him.

When we went to his regular Tuesday visit to the cystic fibrosis clinic, I think Cody covertly wore his heaviest pair of boots and secreted a hefty roll of quarters in his pockets to disguise his weight loss. His diminishing lung function results were chalked up to a slight, impending sniffle and Cody smacked the side of the machine, asking when the last time it'd been serviced was.

When his wonderfully attentive medical team suggested it might be time for another hospital-based incarceration,

Cody flatly refused and reassured everyone in the room he had 'everything under control at home'. He lied, and again I kept my pledge to stay mum, while inwardly wanting to turn him in on the spot. The only thing Cody had under control was the party planning; the rest of him was coming unglued, one forced inhale at a time.

I reamed him verbally and made Cody promise on a stack of cats to double-up on his physiotherapy sessions, consume twice his daily intake of high-calorie Ensure Plus and leave the rest of the party planning to me. We both knew inwardly, it wouldn't be enough, but were sticking to our silent conspiracy.

Cody's mom knows when he's not doing well from a mile off. Even when he tries his best false bravado technique on the phone, or via posts on Facebook. Mothers just know this stuff. She pleaded with him to reconsider the event, and again I lied, suggesting Cody and I had things well in hand. No mention was made of lungs or digestive systems.

The party passed with flying colors! Lungs, on the other hand, failed

The party was a complete success, with a half-dozen of his nurses showing up, friends and school chums I'd not laid eyes on in years, and I spent the majority of the time standing over the grill, attempting to feed the masses. Cody's best chums were keen to reload his tequila-based glass, dancing ensued, and I pulled up the rug and sent almost everyone packing at 2 am. Our son played his part to a T, sporting his best threads, downed the chug-a-lug Molotov cocktail for his cake, and danced like there was no tomorrow.

Cody had 'stay-over' guests in every room, and the entire place looked like a war-torn battlefield at eight in the morning. Bodies akimbo on the sofas, the rugs and even I found one of Cody's childhood buddies out cold and curled up on Texas dog's sleep mat. Cody was cooked, fried, diced and beat to a barely breathing pulp.

When I carried him to the car, for our fast-lane trip to the hospital, he could hardly lift himself off the sofa. I asked him if it was worth it, and his labored reply was a very weak, 'Hell yes!' But I could hear the fear in his throat when he said it.

I made Cody another promise during the drive: I promised, not to ever again keep my mouth shut when he was headed for the graveyard. If he pulled out of this nosedive, I was going to ride his ass, send up flairs and put up billboard-sized posters when I saw him sliding.

Chris, Cody's clinical link, took one look at Cody, plopped him into a wheelchair, connected him to an oxygen mask and rang emergency to cut the red tape for his admittance. He was ticked-off, telling Cody he was sometimes an 'ass', and this admittance was way too late in the making. He wheeled Cody himself, schmoozed the admitting nurse, fast-tracked the paperwork and put Cody on a drip, infusing him with meds; all within 15 minutes. I love that guy.

When Cody was installed in his hospital room, Chris said, 'I'll be back later to check in on you Cody and kick your ass, but I won't be the only one on the team who'll be pounding!'

Cody spent the next three weeks in the hospital, and at least two of the pretty nurses who'd attended his party called in 'sick' on the day of his admittance.

Malignant march to the mailbox

I watched Cody walk the short distance to our mailbox on Hollywood Lane this afternoon. He'd spent most of his day in bed, and I could hear him reaching for breath through our wafer-thin walls. He extracted the mail, mostly fliers for house cleaning and real-estate agent propaganda and leaned into the postbox for support. He looked back to the house, judging the distance for the return journey to our front door and leaning heavily into the big front lawn tree. He was catching his breath.

– Journal entry

Helpless, I struggle to be helpful

I've taken to making hot water bottles which I deploy, casually saying I've made one for myself, and just so happen to have a spare to share. Small lies I hope will be forgiven when I approach the pearly gates. Cody's spleen is four times its normal size now and puts monumental pain and pressure on his guts. His liver is rotten and horrifically diseased, so his spleen has been having to step up or shut down, for almost two years now. No matter what stop-gap relief we seek for our son, Cody goes most nights without decent shut-eye. His mom gives him soothing massages, which take the pressure off, and Cody's told me the best catnaps he gets now, are when his mom is here. Sadly, the moment she stops, his sides remind him that he's not likely to get any further relief.

> I cook and flutter about in the kitchen faking a passion for a plateful of American style, crispy-thin bacon. I try and conjure up an appetite in our son who's diminishing by the day. I've taken to wiping every surface twice with a spray which boasts its ability to kill 99.99999% of all germs. I buy six at a time in the grocery.
>
> Cody reads through me like the Christmas window of Macy's and says nothing that might cause me pain. We play this emotional hide-and-seek every day now, Cody being careful with his father, holding me up while he's holding out for a life-changer or a cure. Texas camps outside Cody's bedroom door, protecting him the best he can.

CHAPTER 19

Are They Kidding? New Lungs and a Liver?

Cody had, with the advice, council and consideration of his CF and diabetes team, elected to try for a liver and lung transplant; the complexities of a triple-organ transplant scared the crap out of me, and his loved ones, although nobody was talking about it openly. The statistical odds were enough to rob any parent of sleep, yet Cody's positive approach, and his insistence on living his life to the fullest, mandated this path for him. He was more often the guy telling his dad, 'Relax old man, it's all going to be just fine!'

I believed him, and I believed in him. Ya gotta just love this guy.

Life on hold

*Try it sometime. Get yourself a straw and breathe
through it for a bit. Perhaps, say, 26 years give
or take. Then, just when you're getting used to it,
making a life of sorts for yourself, reach around with
a free hand, and begin beating your spleen and liver
with a carpenter's claw hammer. Turn the hammer
a few times, so you get the claws working. Do this,
until your spleen is four to five times its normal size,
painfully working overtime for the other organs, which
are failing while you wait for The Call. You'll be pretty
tired after this, so lay down on your clean sheets
and attempt to rest. Don't worry, you're not alone.
You'll have a golden cat curled up like a pillow, and a
small, puppy-like dog stretched across the doorway
to be sure no-one enters without consent. The dog
would be on the bed too, except he moves often, and
every move brings a bit more pain to the effort. Your
parents, loved ones, friends are there in the room with
you, except you can't see them. But I promise you:
they are there. The only distraction you'll have tonight,
is the time it takes to falter to the porcelain white sink
and cough pure, ugly red blood into a plastic cup so
full to the top that you can no longer get the words to
come, or cry for help ...*

– Note in a bottle

I'm cowardly when it comes to changes

When Cody was confronted with the fact that if he didn't
act soon, his options would alter his longevity, I challenged

him to stay on his current path. At first I tempted him with the notion that if it's not broken, why go out of our way to change it. The old, a bird in hand is worth two in the bush notion. When Cody was first delivered this news, he was in relatively good shape, his lung function was not horrific, and although his liver and spleen were 'temperamental', he was getting out of the sack every morning, doing stuff, and living. Mind, he was spending up to four hours each day with postural drainage, physical therapy, guzzling energy and nutritional cartons of chocolate glug, and dropping up to 40 enzyme tablets a day.

'Prof', Cody's doctor, and the medical team at Westmead Hospital had warned us all (his mom, siblings and me in the meeting in a circle, Cody at its center) that things would start deteriorating rapidly from that point on. It was statistically the way things go with cystic fibrosis and diabetes double-punches. Textbook deteriorations, all pointing down like a snowball on a winter mountainside. We sought a third opinion, and I recall getting the 'good news' from a separate clinic, confirming that at that time Cody's liver was functioning close to normal, and it was their opinion that he did not need a new liver. I posted the good news on Facebook, with Cody happy sitting atop a chair, surrounded by massive wooden Christmas soldiers. Fear was driving me to reach for reasons to leave things alone, until Cody put me in my place. 'Dad, relax. I've got this and it is what I want to do. The thought of being able to run, and just breathe, and see everyone without this hanging onto me ... Even *if* I only get one good year out of it, it will be the very best year of my life. Stand with me.

Mom's totally aboard with the munchkin and Dylan. Love you Dad. Let's get this thing done.'

I weep, again. And wonder where this young man finds the strength to hold up his loved ones, and complete strangers among his army of 'cystas' and 'fibros' and reach for a better place. My fears stem mostly from having to put my family's future in the hands of others, where I have virtually no control over the outcome. I'm simply a bystander, anxious, filled with fears, and at the mercy of someone else's skills, or sleight of hand. I'd had Bridget support me fully when I'd elected to leap from one entrepreneurial ledge to another, with total support. And I'd always felt in command of the changes and strived even harder to avoid disappointments. I'd happily paint the entire house by myself rather than leave the trim-work in the corners to someone else.

> *Truth is, I'm scared to tremors at the notion of Cody's plans for a transplant. We seem to be going along just OK, and fear of the unknown if we take this path keeps me without sleep. Are we better off in this treading-water position, or running the risk of another set of organs, when longevity rates are not encouraging? I think his medical team is totally premature, putting this notion in our heads now. If it's not fully broken, I think we should leave it alone. I try to lead Cody in this, saying things like 'Don't let anybody bully you, or push you into anything you don't want to do son! Tell them to all get f*••ed if that's what you want to say! You seem as scared as I am about pulling new organs out of the baggie now. From where I sit, you're doing just fine as you are at the moment.'*

*The fact is change scares the shite out of me now. I
fret over the smallest of unknowns.*

– Journal entry

It's been a very, very hard year

When I really need to let go, I dump a lot on my siblings and
my 'brothers-by-other-mothers'. I know in advance my copy
will not be shared, and there is someone I love who's 'got
my back', even if they're not nearby, or we don't see each
other often.

Cody was now just treading water and waiting for the
call to action on his path to a liver and lung transplant. He
continued to be my hero, an anchor for us all. I knew he was
in perpetual pain, even though he poorly tried to pretend for
my sake it wasn't so bad. I'd curtailed my travel and gave
away my overseas writing commissions and public relations
contracts to stick close to home base on Hollywood Lane.
'The call' could come at any moment and Bridget, the
kids and I non-verbally created a battle plan for when that
happened. When the call came, we were all going to be
emotional Molotov cocktails.

Throw money at it! Fast-track the legal eagles and just get on with it!

When the CF team told Cody he was going to need the
transplants, our only statistically safe option in Oz was to
move full-on to Brisbane where the dual-transplant team
there boasted the best survival odds. This would have meant
uprooting Cody from his kinship group and family – who

play a massive part in making any major transplant attempt successful. The stats are staggering for survival rates if loved ones are on hand for both the lead-up and recovery phases.

We spent the better part of a year working alongside the medical teams locally, as they made a marriage between the very best lung and liver transplant teams in Sydney, which practiced in hospitals on opposite sides of the city, and then, finding a third hospital willing to host both crews for the operating theatre. This sounds insane, but without this parlay, patients would be theoretically cracked open in one hospital's operating theatre, then transported across town to the other transplant team by ambulance for the other organ – the mortality rate has to be horrific. Cody's transplant would be the first joint venture of its kind in Australia, and the hope was to make it work for future dual transplant procedures locally.

We had numerous 'dry runs' to ensure that his procedure could be done under one roof, and Cody, Bridget and I felt we'd gone down the right path. Practice makes perfect.

When Cody elected to go on the transplant list, it was as if his CF team had a crystal ball: in fact, what they had on hand were all the alarming statistics about Cody's rapidly escalating number of admissions, the telltale decrease in lung function and recovery, the painful swelling of his spleen and the fast-lane aggression of his liver disease only pointing in one, significantly sad downward direction. They were spot-on to suggest Cody start the process of seemingly endless tests and paperwork when they did.

The process was a journey undertaken by Cody's family and friends. We spoke with one voice, attended seemingly countless interviews and evaluations, toted coffee cups to Cody's side while he filed in seemingly endless forms, and was poked or prodded by some of the best transplant teams on the planet. Cody's would be a very rare marriage between two remarkable transplant teams, a test case that would allow doctors from a public hospital to operate in the theatre of a private one. The lung transplant team would take nine hours for the new lungs, followed by the liver team. Cody would be in the operating room for over 14 hours from tip to toe before he was brought to the intensive care unit.

As Cody's need for two good lungs and a viable liver progressed, his own organs began to fail him. His workload decreased, and he could no longer sustain a three-day commute and work week. This took a toll on him and affected his headspace as well as self-esteem and independence-oriented bank balance. His enlarged spleen caused immense pain, and nothing seemed provide much relief. Unable to sleep, Cody simply stayed up for nights on end, watching episodes of TV programs where the characters were out to win the world. He dreamed of having the energy to be Ari Gold in the Hollywood-based *Entourage*, or the well-suited lads from *Mad Men.* Cody dreamed of wearing custom-built threads and shoes, driving fast cars, and throwing money at beautiful women. The reality was, just moving a fraction of an inch drove molten spikes deep into his sides.

Broken arrow – promises unkept come back to haunt me

I made a promise to my son, with anger lodged in my throat, saying I would never again allow him to get so close to the edge without dragging him backwards. Even if it meant he wouldn't forgive me for doing it. I broke that promise, only because he asked me to join his conspiracy rather than put his life on hold.

Cody *insisted* on being there on the starting/finish line for the major fundraising event, the 65K 4 65 Roses run – smiling, frisky, and supportive. And giving … again, giving. I have one of those folding camp chairs tucked in behind the inflated starting line arches. Cody, decked out in his Captain America gear sits there, coughing up gooey-green plugs of mucus into a plastic cup. As Cody's co-conspirator, I alert him when I see CF families and friends approach the finish line, so he has time to step, smile widely, shake hands, and hug the kids and grandparents, and absolutely anyone else that steps into his arms.

> *Cody insists on doing this event, and I've reluctantly promised to be a part of the deception. I drive through the drizzle, as Cody does three nebulizers in the car, spilling small rivulets of fire-engine red into a sputum cup. He's hiding the contents from me, covering each with a cloud of Kleenex. I know without looking what's in there, and should be running red lights, diverting for the hospital.*
>
> *'Relax old man, I've got this,' he says to reassure me.*

At the event I guiltlessly roll over three orange obstacle cones placed across the path to get our Cody closer to the starting line, help him into the Captain America outfit and then leave him to work his magic while I park a few miles off. Over 1400 people are participating, and they all seem eager to park – most of them 'Love Someone With CF'.

I race back to my son in now-soggy Topsiders, with a discreetly hidden apothecary of inhalers, enzymes, EpiPen and other tools. He'll need them to keep up the facade. Cody uses them all, needs them all to 'just breathe', out of sight of the cameras, walkers, and crew. Three hours later, I get the nod of exhaustion from my Cody, and race to retrieve the car to the footpath. I tell the fluoro-vested guard I've got four folding-tables to load into the trunk. It's expedient to continue to tell lies. The path monitor has replaced the three squished orange cones I'd guiltlessly wounded earlier, and once out of sight, our Cody collapses into the car for the ride to the emergency room. We learn later, the walk raised over $525,000. Cody insists we don't 'go public' with his hospital admission for a few days: he doesn't want folks to think the event had anything at all to do with his landing back in the slammer.

– Journal entry, 2017

Dad, you're, prone to exaggeration!

I've learned a little trick that I apply to my life. When I catch a fish, I hold it well out in front of me to the lens. It exaggerates the size of the catch. I'm doing the same thing in my daily life, giving the illusion that I'm solid and large and with lots of gusto in my gills still. But it's not true; I'm scared shitless most of the time, on tender hooks emotionally. Even when everything is going along well, I'm peeking behind me, sure, something or someone is going to leap out of the bushes and impale me. I've been feeling like this for months

Dry runs, failed starts, lead-ups and false hopes

Christmas Day 2016 was like no other Christmas we've ever celebrated. We did up Cody's hospital room, plagued the corridors of the fifth-floor ward with fake snowflakes, and forced the nursing staff pals to wear Santa caps, and mistletoe-toe garnished headgear! I fired up my massive, big-bellied Weber grill at 5 am and cooked a turkey, a crackling pork roast and a honey-ham on the front lawn of Hollywood Lane, burning alien-like circles in the new grass. And Bridget, my sisters Cathy and Anne both made side dishes that included Cath's double-baked potatoes, while beautiful Bridget did the creamed cauliflower and salads alongside Hayley. We fed the entire ward, with doggie bags bulging for everyone when it was done. It was our very first year in Cody's 27 years on the planet that we'd had to spend this holiday in the hospital, and I can honestly say it was one of the best. His nurses found excuses to pop in and revel with us. We'd send them all home with a small banquet box of eats and treats. That's just how Cody's team rolled.

During our traditional after-meal game of charades, one of Cody's nurses from another wing of the ward arrived, asking Cody for his height and weight. It seemed an odd question, considering he'd only been measured and weighed a few hours earlier. Its significance didn't become apparent until later in the day. Unknown to us, the transplant team had notified the RNs to get Cody's vitals discreetly: they might just have a 'perfect match' for a pair of lungs and a new liver. Hours later Cody got the call to get ready; tragedy for another family on Christmas Day could possibly deliver a perfect match for him.

Everything went into overdrive after Cody put the phone down. An ambulance was ordered to shift our son from one hospital to the transplant venue 25 miles (40 kilometres) off, and none of us knew how to feel or react to the news and what to say. Fear of the unknown is a powerful force. Cody broke the ice, saying he was going to have a quick shower and a shave – he didn't want to come out of surgery with a three-day growth on his chin! It broke the swelling of emotion for us all.

Cody had already made *positive* plans for what his life was going to be like in a few days' time. Again, Our Cody was leading us, helping us by example. If he could see the good things on the other side of the transplant, we were very tearfully happy to follow.

None of us could have guessed it but the harvested organs were just not right for Cody. Cody has had to stand down on two occasions now. Out of respect for the donor family, the surgeons never provide a great deal of detail about why they are aborting a transplant; they just optimistically support for the notion that the next time, in time, will be the right time.

Heart-rending for one family, we need a horrific tragedy to occur for ours

I spent a good deal of time in the game parks of East Africa, wanting to write like Hemingway, live on the edge with every emotional pore open, and grab all the goodness I could get. My favorite of all the Maasai Mara's animals were the graceful and gentle giraffes. Those eyelashes and long limbs would be envied on any red carpet in Hollywood. On the other end of my passion for the place, were the ugly, bastardly buzzards and vultures. I detested these animals, feathered to resemble undertakers in long-tailed tuxedos. They'd wait impatiently for an animal to lose the strength to fight, and then hop in to tear into the poor creature as it lay dying, scattering organs and flesh everywhere. On one occasion, I'd been reminded by Dr Lawrence Frank, whom I was helping with his Earthwatch expedition to study spotted hyenas that my passion was noteworthy, but this drama was just in keeping with the cycle of life. I'd wanted to load the rifle and slaughter the bunch of bastardly birds as they hopped about with red beaks and entrails dangling everywhere.

Waiting for another family to go into an emotional nosedive, awaiting good matches for our son, I felt as if I were constantly waiting to fall into the abyss. I'd become a lappet-faced vulture. I slept less than poorly, if at all, for many weeks after the second false alarm, praying to the unknown that my Cody would be okay when I visited the hospital the next morning. I knew, without anyone saying it, our son was not going to have any life at all left in him that he deserved. If and when he was discharged to come home.

I try to keep it all in but my need to breathe is making it impossible. My inhales are frighteningly shallow, and my heart rate is rapidly increasing. Higher and higher to the point where I not only hear it pounding like a sub-woofing speaker in my ears, but I can see it in the bathroom mirrors. I feel the gurgling rumble of blood as it makes its way to a cough and then bluurrrgh ... blood is all I see over a white sink and tiles. Bright, fresh, red blood. Lots and lots of it. I'm in full petrified panic and everything gets faster until it's a serious battle to stop the blood on the tiles. My dad tells me he's called the ambulance and I can only nod to suggest it's a very, very wise idea. I overhear him on the phone to Mom. He's scared shitless but tries to pretend calm. Mom's going to meet us there, she's leaving 'now-now'. I'm still leaking blood into a bucket on the way to Westmead. Dad's in the front telling the driver how to drive, and my very switched-on paramedic in the back has done heaps to calm me. She's on the phone, reading my email for emergencies as we go. 'Sorry driver, we're changing destinations ... they're waiting for us at Westmead. Fastest route possible, please!' Our driver never stopped once for a light.

– Cody, journal entry, 1 am admission

I cry re-reading Cody's entry because I *know* the decision the nurse made from the back of the ambulance, against protocol, and the agreement of the ambulance driver to bend the rules and divert to Westmead saved our son's life. Cody's lungs were flooding with blood and, unable to speak, he had the clearest head, and was able to show the nurse a memo from his CF team on his phone. He was given it only the week before, in the highly unlikely event he should ever be unable to speak for himself. When we shifted direction, running lights and speeding to the medical team who knew my son, I could feel the vice grip of his petrified hand in mine soften. I followed his lead. I tried my hardest to appear calm. I don't know how she did it, but his mother was there when our ambulance arrived, standing alongside a medical team who already knew our son. Admissions let me look after the paperwork, and Cody took his mother's hand. I later wept openly in the parking lot for what was likely to happen next.

False bravado

Cody, his family and I would talk about how things were at home, and how they'd be when he came home from the hospital this time, but I think we all knew already, it was the false bravado barking. He'd already suffered two 'false alarms' for an organ donor, and with each failed attempt, his condition deteriorated even more that any of us could have anticipated. With the last massive bleeding episode in his lungs, he was simply treading water on a hospital bed, hoping for a miracle. The nurses on the fifth-floor ward knowingly looked the other way if I or his mother chose to spend the night in a chair alongside his bed. Visiting hours for us were unspoken. We could come and go any time we needed to be with our son. One morning when I arrived to swap places with Bridget, I could see the story in her eyes. Her arms folded across her chest to hold herself together, red eyes from tears she didn't care to share.

I once watched a lung-shot wildebeest, not knowing it was already walking dead, try to return to the herd and graze. The foam-red bubbles leaking from its chest seemed to frighten the others in the herd and they kept moving away. We followed the herd, with the dead-walking wildebeest trailing farther and farther behind, for over an hour before we were able to finally put the animal down with respect. I couldn't get that fucking image out of my head, no matter what I tried. Getting drunk was not an option – I had to be ready and able to drive, and hold loved ones and say 'everything's going to be all right'. Even when I knew it was a lie.

Cody's wonderful brother Dylan was in the USA, doing a 22-gig tour with his band Ruth Carp and the Blowfish. When he heard his brother was called for the transplant, he phoned to ask me for help to get him the fastest flight home. Cody took the phone, which had been on speaker, from my hand and reminded his lifelong wingman that he was not to put life on hold or alter his course. Cody said, 'I've got this Dylan. Keep going bro!'

Both of the earlier transplant calls occurred, almost like clockwork during national celebrations and holidays. We were forewarned that this would be the case, as tragedy strikes harder and with more frequency over celebration periods. I found myself looking at the calendar, determining the time gap between holidays, three-day weekends and national events. I'd turned into a vulture, circling on the thermals for a miracle to appear on the horizon.

Third time lucky. Cody called at 6 am to say he'd got the private number call from St Vincent's Hospital, and this time it looked like a full-on green light. The call that changed us all!

It was the number he had for the transplant unit and he knew that when they called, he would go, headed into a liver and lung transplant that would change, or end his life. Cody had a caller ID on his mobile phone, and it simply read: 'The Call!'

> *It rang the other evening, and we sat watching the phone vibrate on the tabletop. It rang five times before Cody answered it. It was a false alarm. Neither of us knew whether to be relieved or disappointed. Cody keeps a 'ready pack' by our front door, and an envelope sealed there that I'm not to open until he goes under the knife.*
>
> *– Journal entry, 2016*

On the third call to action, I was at home and I said I'd tear out to the hospital to help him pack up his room. He'd been 'recovering' for over two weeks from a massive lung hemorrhage, when he said, 'Dad, Dad! STOP! There's no time. By the time you get here, I'll already be in the ambulance, headed for my new liver and lungs. Just meet me there, along with Mom and Hayley!'

His loving nurses at Westmead Hospital packed him up pronto and minutes later, Cody posted a live Snapchat with his paramedic from the ambulance, capturing the siren in the backdrop as they tore through red lights and intersections.

'OK folks, you can hear the sirens in the background, well, it's happening. Hopefully this time around I'll get the new parts I'm needing! I'm ready, and I'm soooo over this waiting thing. I'll be turning my phone and FB stuff over to my kid-sister Hayley, so she's in charge until further notice. This is Captain America of the CF Avengers signing off for now. Good Morning, good afternoon, and good evening! I'll talk to you with the new body parts real soon! Love ya!'

He saluted his audience, smiling. He was confident, and motivated, sure this time he was going to get a pair of new lungs and a liver.

I was emotionally bankrupt and unsure if I could keep up without cracking. I was under instructions from Cody to tread gently on any Cody-condition news I shared. It's called loving censorship. And again, before he went under the knife, he told his family to relax, he had this! I believed him.

The tiniest speck of good news becomes a headline I hold onto like a raft!

When you have a loved one in jeopardy, you hold on tightly to the smallest bit of good news, as if it's a life raft. A smile through an oxygen mask, a squeeze of your hand by your child. I could catalogue the good things I lifted to the top of my awareness when Cody came out of the operating theatre. Both good and bad, I elevated and replayed over and over in my emotional no-man's land. High on the timeline of things that we all clung to were:

> It's all going so well to this point. Your son is taking every third breath with his new lungs, outdoing the 'normal' timeline for the new lungs to begin going; they seem very eager to kickstart. Hours later, he was breathing

entirely on the new lungs, and his doctor who did the
extraction of the lungs, via police escort, and the 14-hour
procedure said the donor lungs were Olympian-quality
examples of great lungs.

– Journal entry

Cody's liver team, sometimes four of them, would climb into cabs for weeks after the five-hour liver transplant, three times a day in cross-town traffic, to check on him, and collaborate with the lung team. They were on 24-hour call, and on one occasion, arrived at 3 am for a joint consultation when Cody began amassing 4 litres of liquid in his body cavity. Over 100 taxi vouchers record the path well-traveled to keep a good grip on Cody's recovery. Worth every kilometre.

My journal entries while Cody's in ICU have tears on 'em

- Cody's spleen celebrated the moment his new liver was attached by shrinking from four times its seriously overstressed self to normal, even while our son was still in the operating theatre.

- Cody is moving his fingers and toes.

- Cody can have clear liquids to drink, and Jello/ jelly. Okay, great, let's get him sparkling water. Oops! No bubbles! He'll puff up like a hot air balloon. Sorry son, we got that bit wrong, but thankfully Bridget asked for clarification.

- Okay Cody, if you can get your head to please have a conversation with your bowels it would help. I never thought I'd get so excited about hearing a fart! Cody's mom and sister did squat-leg exercises with Cody to encourage flatulence and I'm amazed it got his butt-crack working ... and meant we could bypass more tubes and tablets and even dialysis.

- Cody, you're doing well. We're taking one of the four drains we've got in you out tomorrow if you continue on this path.

- I asked: 'Doctor, just how much of this gunk can come out yet?'

- Cody! You've nailed your sugars – you're a glucose poster-boy candidate! Keep up the good work!

- The best liver transplant team in the Pacific happened to be from another hospital but they agreed to commute for our Cody. The team comes two, three, times a day by car to Cody's bedside to examine his progress, and to collaborate with the lung transplant team (also the best in their business!) to compare notes and agree the treatment path. I love these people! And his nurses who tend our son as if he was theirs too. Even Miles, who pushes the beds about the ward, and who helps gently shift Cody and changes bed sheets and pillowcases is a legend in my ledger.

Intensive CARE YOU-knit

Calls and notes, and emails and Skype messages poured in from everywhere. Cody'd given his Facebook page and mobile phone to his sister to tend, but it seemed an overwhelming ask for all the well-wishers who pleaded and needed to know what was happening.

Cody's cousin Meghan in the USA wrote a note, asking for his postal details so she could assemble a package. I replied saying:

> *> Hi Meggler-Peggler!*

> *> I love the notion of a 'care package' for our Cody but I'm just fearful that by the time it arrives he'll hopefully be home sleeping in his own bed! Send packages to him on Hollywood Lane. Oh yeah, send your modest, young and 50-something Uncle Mark some money! The guy, for a three-organ transplant (see 15+ hours in surgery!) is well ahead of recovery for outpatient status.*

> *> Yesterday he told me: 'Get ready old man, I'm coming home' (If he has anything to do with it 'next week'). And besides, they've moved Cody three times already. As he gets stronger, and in need of less attention – ICU, then heightened-care unit, then high-dependency ward, then general ward, and pre-release – it's a bit like a factory in some cases! BUT ... what a new guy they've built! SO: finding him in the hospital is sometimes a challenge for 'surprise visitors' who rock up, and find another fella in the bed Cody had only yesterday.*

> My heart bleeds for the donor's family, whose horrific tragedy of losing such a healthy young person has given our Cody another shot. Cody's been gifted the lungs and whole liver of a top-shelf athlete. His lungs insisted on working within four hours of the operation, and his liver was so eager to go to work, that his spleen, which had been overworked and swollen to four times its natural size, chose to go on vacation while Cody was on the operating table and shrunk to its normal girth – as if it said 'Finally! I got a liver that's doing its job ... I'm taking a little vacation.' (Cody did not have very long on his old lungs. And his liver was diseased and deteriorating for years. I fretted nightly, when he was in the other hospital if I'd find him functioning without help the next morning.)

> His mom, beautiful Bridget, and Hayley have been monumental in his recovery ... at the bedside every single day. Even when they can't be at the bed, they hover.

> On day 3 in ICU, I asked the concerned doctors at the foot of Cody's bed, if Cody's brain needed to have a conversation with any other part of his body to help his recovery, which body part would he be speaking to? The doc said, 'Cody, get your head to talk to your butt-end and bowels. We'd welcome even a good loud fart right now! You're blocked, and we don't want to subject you to another procedure if we can avoid it. Start chatting NOW.'

> Bridget, hearing this offered to use some of her targeted Kahuna therapy techniques, if it might help,

and the doctor said, 'By all means, go for it.' Bridget
and Hayley gently administered knee bends, and other
bowel-loosening techniques to Cody's legs, and a few
hours later, success ... I never thought I'd celebrate the
arrival of a big fart with such excitement! (Pass this note
to your sister Eloise – she'll love the FART, FART bits!)

> Dylan is here too EVERY SINGLE DAY! Even as he
moves around the USA with the band's tour. Cody
reminds me that he's got Dylan right alongside the bed
in his heart. The Captain America Teddy, which I think
has morphed into a Dylan-thing, is never out of arm's
reach!

> OK, enough from TOM!

Cody introduced me as 'TOM' to one of the nurses who actually thought it was my name; I didn't have the heart to enlighten her that my real name is Mark. I wear TOM – 'The Old Man' – with great pride coming from my kids! It's our little inside joke.

Family first!

Cody said he does not know how anyone could get through what he's been through without family. He gives us far too much credit, but I quietly peek through the curtains and see others who get no visitors at all after such life-altering operations. Cody and I began visiting other beds, once his mandate from physiotherapy was to 'get moving often' and my publisher, Fiona at New Holland, gave us a heap of nice books for reading while nice nurses(!) and patients go through the healing process.

Oh yeah, at Cody's orders, I purchased new sandwich presses for this floor as well – a 'must have' according to Captain America, which made him a hospital-wide hero among the nurses and other lock-ups in recovery. He told me not to tell anyone where they came from, but I crossed my fingers when I promised. Later I told him I was forced to say where they came from for 'maintenance'. They had to, by law, put a sticker on everything that got plugged into a socket.

Cough catchers! Fisticuffs on the curb!

On Cody's very first outdoor day post-transplant I nearly came to blows with a wino, decked out in medical scrubs. I'd asked him to kindly remove his cigarette and himself from his nest on the curb right outside the hospital's front doors, posted with the ghostbuster-type signage everywhere banning smoking anywhere, on hospital property. Cody was in the company of a male nurse from ICU, and a hospital ward porter, with his IV drip. Laden with meds, tagging along behind him for the monumental first breaths outside the ICU. Cody had two brand new lungs, and he was very, very keen to use them.

Even after explaining the need for the smoking bloke to stub his smoke, the chap got belligerent and advanced on me, cigarette suspended from the lip, and with clenched fists. In my youth, surrounded by teenaged witnesses I'd have knocked every tooth out of his head without relenting. I had to threaten bodily harm, my rage gaining the upper hand. I have a photograph I took shortly afterwards, my adrenaline still pounding, but it's a bit blurring from the shaking.

Today, it is virtually *impossible* to approach the hospital from any angle or entry point, without seeing Cody on a poster, or billboard, or freestanding sign saying 'Don't even think about it!' I haven't been up on the roof yet, but I think he's up there as well. Hospital security now has pivotal cameras, and an improved PA speaker system at every exit, with a security guard emboldened with a meaningful mission. Gotta problem? Throw money at it.

The air up there!

Cody's long-standing friend. Tommy Danger, who's established the More Than Just Me foundation, tells a story of why he climbs to the thin air peaks, and he always finishes his ascent with the somewhat guilty feeling that he can come down, while leaving CF-loved ones up where the air is thin. Cody suggests that for a feel of what it's like each and every day of a cystic fibrosis life attempt to spend a just a single day breathing through a straw. I posted a video clip, of a young CF woman who after her lung transplant, breathed on her own with new, full lungs. She was overwhelmed with how it felt, to 'just breathe'. When Cody got his new lungs, he asked if they were working, because he no longer had to strain to get his breath! Big smiles.

We need a cure ... and meanwhile, we *need* significant sign-ups for organ donors, please. Are you an organ donor yet? I ask *everyone* I meet now.

Flying higher – our soaring son

Our Cody has taken to the notion that he's now been gifted four more hours, each and every day of his new life, and he has no intention of wasting a single second of it. He goes ahead like a big-top crusading Baptist, preaching redemption to a full house.

> *Cody came home from his medical review yesterday (he's driving himself ... I secretly miss not going along as his bodyguard) saying he could very well be cleared to fly in a month's time! REMARKABLE – from the moth to the butterfly ... and we forget how much the moth has had to go through to get there!*
>
> *– Journal entry, August 2017*

> *I watched this morning, OUR Cody W. Sheehan run at speed, with energy to spare and not a single cough to be heard at the end of the trail ... today was Cody's last 'official' post- transplant session under supervision, in the hospital's gym ... and I'm powerless to express this miracle with words. There are teardrops on my page. Happy ones.*
>
> *– Facebook entry, 16 July 2017*

The *Daily Telegraph* had a photo of our Cody and the Prime Minister on page 3, touting the medical miracle 'marriage' between the best private and public hospital transplant teams working side by side in the very same operating theatre. Cody's earlier transplant options were the USA, or relocating the entire troop Sheehan to Brisbane! Go get 'em Cody ... there are a lot more of your 'cystas' and 'fibros' out there who need ya!

My heart bleeds for him

Cody was up most of the evening, talking to his peers and CF pals. I could only hear bits and pieces through our paper-thin cottage walls, but I knew enough to know that tragedy had struck again, somewhere in our Cody's world. Until a cure is found for cystic fibrosis, Cody and his world will continue to be devastated by the news that others, unable to get organ transplants in time, simply can't hold on, hold out any longer. I wept when Cody told me he'd lost his youngest CF Avenger. He and his family had been hovering on the brink for over two weeks in ICU, praying and hoping for a viable donor kidney. The call never came. The real heartbreaker for our son, is the knowing that he is one of the lucky ones. He got his two bright new lungs and a remarkable full liver just in the nick of time, while other beautiful creatures, and loving families try to sleep on razor blades, hoping and praying for another family's tragedy to save them.

Why me?

I can't presume to know what runs through the mind of my son, but I have been given glimpses. Cody, a bit like the lone survivor of a horrific air crash, seems to ask the unanswerable question of why me? The timing for his miracle transplant came, literally at the eleventh hour. He was waiting in a hospital, with his rotten lungs hemorrhaging already when the call came. It was the third call of its kind, but we all knew if the transplant didn't go ahead, there would be no further runway for our son to use in time.

Meanwhile: I made an entry in my journal, after I arrived one morning to find superhero helium balloons floating in his room, a series of Marvel comics splayed across the hospital bed and a note from our son, saying he was down in the hospital gardens with a brand-new friend. The other CF kid was seven years old, wore a superhero's mask to avoid cross-contamination and he was attempting to show our Cody how he could climb trees. His mom, nearby, tears in her eyes, rolled the stroller with her new, non-CF baby back and forth in the shade. Cody continues to inspire, enlighten and motivate! Parents, other CF kids and one of his CF Avengers-in-training came all the way from the back of Baulkham Hills to spend just an hour with Cody. I'm a very proud papa!

Thank you will never-ever be enough! Cody's letter to the donor

Dear you amazing human being, I officially know nothing about you, but I am indebted to you for the rest of my life. For someone who I will never have the privilege of meeting or knowing I owe you everything because if it wasn't for you, I would not be here to be able to carry out and live for the both of us. I have just graduated my last class in session of transplant rehabilitation and it's quite extraordinary. That's all because of you and your family and for that I can never thank you enough. Gratitude will never be enough, thank you will never be enough, praise will never be enough, there is nothing I can do that will show the extent of my appreciation enough to even come close to the second chance and gift that you have unconsciously, unknowingly provided for me at a most critical hour. Simply put, without you there would be no me and that's as simple and frank

as it gets. I do have a strange feeling that you were
very healthy. I do have a strange feeling that you were
younger and shorter than I am, and they also had a
strange feeling that you may have been female; again,
I can't confirm any of that until I contact your family
lovingly.

If you look back, you'll soon be going that way

This was the note in tonight's fortune cookie from Lees Fortuna restaurant. We have celebrated family milestones there with 'the sword' to cut birthday cake for over 30 years now and counting. Our entire family was around the table. We celebrated Cody's homecoming from a trip to the USA. He'd gone there and home, visited with a fistful of his CF 'cystas' and 'fibros', some of them at their hospital bedsides. He did the 15 hours flying time without an oxygen pump on his lap.

I looked around the table at my handsome family gathered and began to weep openly for all the love I saw there. I've been doing it a lot of late. Mine are welcomed tears of gratitude, and my family looking back at me, simply smiled and understood. Hayley came around the table and bear-hugged her old man. She was weeping as well. I keep two framed posters on my bedroom wall I can see from any perch there. One is a wilted billboard, on now-browned newspaper stock. It has two words on it: Mandela VRY! The other, equally faded has only one word on it: GRATITUDE.

Easter, again

After Cody's successful transplant, I thought I'd heard the last of his nebulizers on Easter Sunday. But Cody developed a chunk of pseudomonas in his nasal passageways, and his proactive team prescribed a week or two of antibiotics to inhale with the mask on again. I heard it doing revs through his bedroom door, which put me on edge again; like turning back the clock. I've pulled up my journals and recall:

> *Lake Powell, Page Arizona. We've been given a*
> *gorgeous suite overlooking the lake and sunshine*
> *bounces off the surface, layered oranges and reds in*
> *the canyon rock look like postcards. Hayley and Dylan*
> *play on the damp grass, while Cody watches, flicking*
> *his hands in anticipation of joining in when he's finished*
> *his mask full of inhalants for the morning. When Cody's*
> *excited he flaps his beautiful hands in the air like he's*
> *attempting to dry them. The lodge's GM is nearby*
> *planting Easter eggs in the shrubbery and under pool*
> *lounges for an Easter-egg hunt for staff and guests.*
> *Dylan will later uncover the egg with the gold bunny*
> *inside, which earns him a full set of plastic golf clubs,*
> *plastic balls and strapped bag which I will have to find*
> *room for in the boot of the rented Lincoln Town Car. It's*
> *the same morning I slam Cody's hand in the car door.*
> *As if this kid hasn't had enough to cry about. On our*
> *way into the South Rim of the Grand Canyon is starts to*
> *snow ...*
>
> *– Journal entry*

CHAPTER 20

Don't Ever Mention the War!

Life moves on, and I've successfully avoided being 'baited' into political side-picking and have largely keep my ideas to myself. This has given me free access to a variety of political hallways without hassle and I've been perfectly happy fence-sitting outwardly until now ... The civil war which has broken out in my America has moved me to tears; I read the heart-reading notice from a kindergarten pal, who publicly told another lifelong pal he was 'a piece of crap for the way he'd voted, and he was no longer welcomed in the home, and was f**king dead to him for as long as he lived'. It was not the first venomous hate notice I'd noticed seeping onto social network pages.

I had to find a way to vent – our Victory Garden Party gave me a shovel for all the shit!

Someone really famous said 'Think globally, act locally'! Like the scene from the flick *Network*, I was becoming the guy in the window, who screamed 'I'm sick of all this crap, and I'm NOT GONNA TAKE IT ANYMORE!'

I created a Facebook 'party line' modeled on the historic Victory Gardens of World Wars I and II, for sharing thoughts and ideas about how to make things better. We seem to have turned over our lives to others: church, union, employer, political 'leaders' and lost the feeling of being able to accomplish a better place for ourselves and the people whom we care for. Change starts at the bottom, and has the capacity to grow, but many of us feel helpless.

The idea of a Victory Garden extends far beyond the backyard: it is more about making a positive difference in your own life, and that of the people whom you care about that surround you. Making a difference in our own 'backyard' – I can't do much for global warming, or save the whales but I do, put $10 in the pot when they come to our front door. Meanwhile, I try to focus on the people, and the things I *can* make positive things happen for within my community and my family. Imagine if we all did this ...

FDR had a clear view of the future. Even in times when we feel helpless, frustrated about playing any part at all, or making any measurable difference I'm reminded of his fabulous notion of 'Victory Gardens': making things happen in our very own backyards, or alongside the footpath, heartwarming stories of grandparents growing tomatoes in apartment flower boxes in the hope their grandsons might get a meal across the ditch in a trench somewhere.

My Victory Garden has almost, nothing to do with gardening

I'm a bit of a late-bloomer myself. Last year, we gifted perhaps 80,000 seeds to anyone who asked for them; I think a fair few, still, remain in the packets. They can't ever bear fruit if they never find their way to the ground. I've taken the liberty of late of just tossing at random, seeds into the backyard patch, and applying water on occasion. Although I don't know what the hell everything growing in there is I've already harvested some remarkable veggies. You never know unless you take a shot at it! Sorta like, *life*?

In 1943, 20 million Victory Gardens were producing 8 million tons of food. Almost one-third of the entire American food harvest for that season! That very same year, 1943, Golden Gate Park in San Francisco boasted over 200 Victory Gardens – baseball fields and public playgrounds became community garden spots. The emotional uplifting given to all of those too young or too old to fight on the frontlines can't be measured: 'I'm too old to sign up, but my grandson might just get a good meal in France tonight. Those are not *just* tomatoes you're holding in your hands!' People were able to make a difference by focusing on the things they could change. Perhaps a message for our times? Don't worry about the things we can't alter; focus on the ones we can. Apply this notion to everyday living today and the same remains true: make a difference in your own patch. Just add water, care, and maybe a bit of sunshine in a smile. Without knowing it, my family, Cody's journey with cystic fibrosis to his triple-organ-transplant are all, in a way, my Victory Garden.

Wine turns the idiot into a wise man, and the wise man into and idiot

I drank my way through the youth of all our children. And while I'd been contemplating an end to my drinking career, I was holding out for a sign of some kind. A lightning bolt of revelation, or some yet-unknown trigger than would lead me to sobriety. My friend Hunter once told me over the backyard barbecue, he had a 'pal' who had real issues with alcohol abuse, and they made a pact: both would simply stop, and if the need or desire to have a shooter ever arose, they'd call each other first to share the news. Hunter was over six years 'dry', and never once got a call. I tried this myself years later, with someone I loved more than life itself, and it backfired on us both badly. Instead of helping us to stop, we supported each other as we stumbled into the next, New York bar.

Not every sow, has a silver ear?

If I went hunting for an upside to my increased intake of alcohol, I could always fall back on the notion that it was research. I began writing 'The Underground Alcoholic's Handbook' in my spare time! Complete with inebriated insights. I occasionally got confused about who the audience might be for it, but the words poured out of me like the gold nectar in a Johnnie Walker Blue bottle. I just let my observations from under the table spill out. One day when I have the time I'll go back and look at the slurred words in it fully.

A turning point for lifting my grog game came when Bridget challenged me after one particular event. I needed assistance to get to the bedsheets, being three sheets to the wind before our house guests left. Bridget said, she did not want any of our kids, to ever see either of us slurring our words. I was, by my own definition, a functional alcoholic, who on occasion, was far less than functional.

For Bridget, a truly careful sipper, this would not be a challenge. I had to learn to slow up or go underground with my grog. I chose camouflage over compromise and learned the drinker's creed of covering up with many deceptions.

I always said I'd much rather give up grog than my very cold 2% milk. In 1972, I returned to my hometown of Manhasset, New York, abandoning the best 'job' a fella could ever ask for in East Africa. I missed my family immensely, but I might have remedied that by sending them airline tickets, but the prospects of ever getting anything more advanced that long-life milk in Uganda were next to none. The Tuskers beer was brilliant, but I was addicted to the cold white. I missed my cold, very cold 2% milk.

When Cody's transplant advisor David told our son his longevity rate would leap if he avoided alcohol in regular doses, Cody responded by saying he had no intention of drinking grog again any year soon. Cody was never much of a drinker before his transplant, but with the statistical data confronting him, he was keen to just go cold turkey.

I seized the opportunity to join him, saying that when Cody next wanted to take a taste, he could call me, or tap me on the shoulder and I'd join him. No big deal, no call to arms or pledge made to honor the date, just a verbal feel-good for me as Cody's father. Something we could engage in together.

It turned out I'd been covertly looking for a good reason to actually stop the grog, if for nothing else, to prove to myself I could.

I felt fabulous from the very start. Just declaring my sobriety silently, for myself. About four months after my son and I went into grog-free mode I got a call from Cody. 'Dad, I'm going to do the toast at Grace's wedding with a fully-charged flute of champagne, and just wanted to let you know.' I said thanks for the heads-up, but if it was okay with him, I'd just prefer to keep going and see how long I might run. After all, I'd saved hundreds of dollars, shed significant kilos, and could once again close the buttons on my pants without sucking in. I felt fabulous, so I was just going to keep going. I've lost track now of when exactly we tossed in the bar-rag but it's not even important.

I hardly ever steal the *Reader's Digest* from the doctor's reception anymore

Yesterday, while I was waiting to hear firsthand the GP's good news on my blood test results, smooth blood pressure and weight drop, I played with my calculator. I'd have stolen another copy of the *Reader's Digest,* but the receptionist was onto me from an earlier visit. So I played out the numbers on my sobriety and they told another nice story. I could easily peek back at my credit card bills for the grog shop, and occasional pub spending: If I spent an average of $84 a week on household grog, or drinks in the pub it totaled more than $4300 a year. Back that spend up over the past 20 years for the fun of numbers, and I'd gulped nearly $90,000 – forgetting all the gallons of SEG (someone else's grog) I'd ingested at significant open-bar functions, parties and free shouts.

Feeling frisky, I sent the kids all the grog savings, and both Hayley and Dylan countered with, 'Dad! That's way too much I'm sending some back!' My reply was simple: 'I won the lottery kiddo! Enjoy it!' And I had: not drinking is a new flight plan I have no intention of altering. I can't recall ever as an adult feeling better. My clothes fit. I'm clear headed every morning. I like the bloke in the mirror. If I have to say 'I'm sorry' the next day, it's not because I can't recall what I said.

My friend Hunter's commitment to stop drinking in support of a friend has stuck in my recollection for nearly 30 years now and counting.

I've got no plans to celebrate an alcohol-free anniversary. I've already lost track of the month, and soon, the year I elected to step off the stuff. Just don't even think about getting me to give up my cold, very cold 2% milk. My only regret on the matter is, that I could have done it earlier.

CHAPTER 21

Superhero | Cody |

A few years ago, before his transplant, Cody could hardly get into his Captain America costume without help, yet he mustered a brave and happy face for the starting gun. Only a handful of the 1500 folks there knew he could hardly walk 20 yards with his dying lungs. I had hidden a chair off to the side for him to rest, out of sight of the crowd who'd come to run alongside my son for a CF cure … and then … In 2018 you couldn't hold *our* Cody W. Sheehan back, as he tested his two powerful donor-gifted lungs alongside his beautiful 'gym wife' and pal. I made sure I didn't cry in front of my son each time he crossed the lap lines: I was not the only guy who shed a few grateful tears for his second chance. I was one proud and happy 'old man'.

Run for your life … and for the ones who can hardly walk at all

Tears here. My friend Jack elected to walk and perhaps run for a bit alongside Cody in the CF 65 Roses fundraiser. He ran it the year before, powering through, while Cody was propped up on the finish line to encourage others, while his lungs were bleeding the life out of him slowly. This time around, Jack had survived some serious medical plagues of his own and came to the finish line in tears. He was jacketed in perspiration and pulling hard for every breath.

Jack's tears were those of unbridled joy, for he'd just had Cody, garbed as Captain America and his fabulously fit 'gym wife' Cairyn blast past him *running*. Knowing he'd pay the piper for a full week afterwards, Jack vowed to do another lap of the course. Later he said it was one of the most satisfying accomplishments of his life. Like my friend, Cody has inspired and enlightened hundreds, perhaps closer to thousands of people with his passion for life, his dedication to a higher service, and I wish him well for his continued laps around the track. I too, have been uplifted, and made better by my wonderful son Cody.

As I write, I have to confess I have, never-ever, in my adult life felt this fine. I slide out of bed at 5 am now, keen to make the most of every extra moment I've been given as a gift. And my loved ones have by example given me the magical manifest that makes it all possible. Cody's journey has tested me, and it has rewarded me with so much good that there has never been an instrument fine enough to measure it.

Like Aesop's fables, if I have a dangly bit at the end, a moral to the story to share, it must be in the notion that I am the master of my fate. The captain of my soul. Like the 'Invictus' prose of William Ernest Henley, I shall get out of bed every day that I have been 'gifted' and try …

> *Out of the night that covers me,*
> *Black as the pit from pole to pole,*
> *I thank whatever gods may be*
> *For my unconquerable soul.*
>
> *In the fell clutch of circumstance,*
> *I have not winced nor cried aloud.*
> *Under the bludgeonings of chance,*
> *My head is bloody, but unbowed.*
>
> *Beyond this place of wrath and tears*
> *Looms but the Horror of the shade,*
> *And yet the menace of the years*
> *Finds, and shall find, me unafraid.*
>
> *It matters not how strait the gate,*
> *How charged with punishments the scroll,*
> *I am the master of my fate:*
> *I am the captain of my soul.*

We've come a long, long way and there are still billions of phlegm-filled breaths to take, gallons of ugly, to-the-very-brim septum cups to discard, and millions of enzymes for CFers to swallow along the track. Yet, every day good people get closer to the cure. And knowing this, gives me great strength. I try to emulate my son Cody's gusto each day of his crusade and I try, to follow his example, grateful for every breath.

Let 'CF' stand for 'cure found!' is our single mantra, our constant chant around Hollywood Lane now.

I too love your loved one – you gave us our son, and a second chance

Dear loved ones,

My heart bleeds for your loss; I cannot fathom the depth of pain, heart-shattering agony you have had to endure. There is simply no type of condolence that can carry your pain, your suffering away. I just wanted you to know that from here on out, for every single day of my life, I will honor you for your gift to me and my family. Our son, OUR Cody is alive, and doing so very well because of your selfless, gift. Cody also has told me repeatedly that he loves your incredible, wonderful, gift of life. I've spent a good deal of my life hovering around, and making things happen with words. And none of them, are strong enough, or emotionally sufficient to even begin to let you know that your loved one, is now also ours. Cody's dad

A message from Cody

*I've watched my father quietly, from the sidelines while
he struggled with this book. Both he and my mother
have always been there for me. The very least I could do
for him, would be to help free him from writing an ending
for my story. I've got many, many more chapters to
complete, and I've taken my old man off the hook saying
the next telling of my tale will be from my pen. I've said
it before, and I'll repeat it here again: My name is Cody
Sheehan! Keep your eyes peeled. I'm headed your way!*

– Cody

| Acknowledgements

There has never been a tool created that can measure my gratitude

Years ago now, when I'd finished *America Over Easy* our 'know before you go' travel guide, I filled the final two pages from margin to margin with the names of the wonderful people and places that helped me along the way. Even then, I managed to somehow neglect and leave some fabulous folks un-hugged on paper.

Listing the hundreds upon hundreds of caring people who have helped *Cody & I* come this far is an absolutely impossible undertaking. Emotionally, I add to it hourly.

I am so thankful to Bridget for saying yes to being married, and for keeping a promise she made on the day our son was diagnosed to never ever give up. I can count on one hand the number of days she took for herself while we raised Cody, Dylan and Hayley to adulthood. The image in the picture section of this book is spot on: CF doesn't come with a manual, it comes with a mother who refuses to give up.

I've been blessed from birth with a remarkable family. My five wonderful siblings and I were raised by an exceptional duo of parents who taught us we were capable of being and doing anything we desired if we wanted it enough. I will one day write the story of what it was to grow up surrounded by love: I am the luckiest kid I've ever known.

I've sadly done the eulogy now for two remarkable people: Chris Newman and Nick Tarsh, who quietly fought alongside Bridget and me to keep our family in Australia. Against significant odds. When the corporate bean counters said the Sheehans were toting 'too much baggage', both Chris and Nick advised them to start counting. RIP, you altered our lives in the very best of ways.

There are simply not enough pages to thank all the medical teams and dedicated nursing staff who own a piece of our son. I once took a photo of Cody post his triple-organ transplant, surrounded by a bevy of his nurses, saying, 'Thank you, you each own a piece of my son!' We roared with laughter over which bits they were bidding on! If you're reading this in surgical scrubs, you already know I'm thanking you with the hugest of hugs. You know who you are.

On the night Cody's lungs began to pour forth cups of raw blood, the ambulance nurse made a choice that saved our son's life. Cody, unable to speak, handed the paramedic his phone with a protocol that was created, only the week before by 'Prof' and Lucy from Westmead Hospital.

Reading it, she pleaded with the driver to shift course and divert protocols, and fly with haste to a different emergency room. Cody's team, alerted by this same nurse, were waiting for us when we arrived. I've no doubt she saved my son. Cody's quick-thinking Lucy and Doc Middleton's foresight, and the duo in the ambulance changing course, made it possible to keep Cody breathing until …

Every well-planted tent needs good, solid anchors holding down the corners. Doc Morton at Randwick Children's Hospital was proactive at leading the way for us finding new, innovate ways to keep Cody healthy, enlightening Bridget about new techniques and medications.

At the other three corners of Cody's metaphorical tent we had Prof. Middleton and the two Davids. We discovered Dr David Abelson as Registrar at St Vincent's Hospital. David was, for me, a remarkable security blanket. I was so traumatized (make that scared shirtless) at the notion that things would not end well with Cody's election to list for the transplant, and David's confidence gave the face of humanity to the team that was either going to take or save our son's life. I slept better with David at the end of Cody's bed, echoing Cody's reminder to 'Relax old man, we've, got this!'

Our other David, guru of most things liver-related, was anchored at Royal Prince Alfred Hospital. Dr David Bowen quietly oozed confidence and put us at ease with every encounter. Some people can just make me settle down; Doctor Bowen is one of them. When he leans back in his chair and laughs, I laugh louder.

Max Perkins, good friend and editor for both Ernest Hemingway and F. Scott Fitzgerald at Scribner's in New York, commented once about just how many front cover renderings he had to suggest before he felt comfortable he had got the 'right feel' for a book's cover. *The Great Gatsby* took 11 tries, while *The Old Man and the Sea* required 16! Max refused to let the books loose until he was happy. Our lovely Fiona Schultz of New Holland Publishing told Cody and me she was up to 58 possible front-cover renderings of this book ... and she was still counting! Cody and I are so very lucky to have her breathing the same air alongside us. I've never encountered a more remarkable or dedicated publisher, which goes a long way to explaining why I count her as a close and loving friend.

Fiona's team have been nothing short of monumentally kind to us. Lesley Pagett, Fiona's long-time PA and friend, reads me like a book. Liz and Warren and Arlene, Chris, Yolanda and Catherine, possess the patience of a pack-full of saints. I've been well nested with New Holland for almost 30 years now. Fiona has watched our kids grow. I'm grateful she continues to care.

Most of all, I thank Cody. My son. He gave me every good reason to get my ass off the mattress, every fine moment to smile without obvious reason, and re-taught me the true value of living; even if it meant breathing through a straw. I am blessed beyond any instrument for ever measuring.

Keep your eyes peeled please! Cody's coming ...

First published in 2021 by New Holland Publishers
Sydney • Auckland

Level 1, 178 Fox Valley Road, Wahroonga, NSW 2076, Australia
5/39 Woodside Ave, Northcote, Auckland 0627, New Zealand

newhollandpublishers.com

A record of this book is available from the National Library of Australia.

ISBN 9781760793807

Group Managing Director: Fiona Schultz
Publisher: Fiona Schultz
Project Editor: Liz Hardy
Designer: Yolanda La Gorcé
Production Director: Arlene Gippert

Printed in Australia

10 9 8 7 6 5 4 3 2 1

Keep up with New Holland Publishers:
NewHollandPublishers
@newhollandpublishers

US $19.99